Everyday Miracles

Everyday Miracles

Stories from Life

F. FORRESTER CHURCH

 A Cornelia & Michael Bessie Book

HARPER & ROW, PUBLISHERS, *New York*
Cambridge, Philadelphia, San Francisco, London,
Mexico City, São Paulo, Singapore, Sydney

Portions of this work originally appeared in the *Chicago Tribune* and *Harvard Divinity Bulletin.*

FIRST EDITION

Designed by Sidney Feinberg

Library of Congress Cataloging-in-Publication Data

Church, F. Forrester.
  Everyday miracles.

  "A Cornelia & Michael Bessie book."
  Includes index.
  1. Meditations.   2. Church, F. Forrester.
I. Title.
BV4832.2.C5295   1988   242   88-45173
ISBN 0-06-015976-6

88 89 90 91 92 CC/HC 10 9 8 7 6 5 4 3 2 1

To Twig and Nina

Contents

Preface   xv

I. FAMILY TIES

1. A Brush with Death—and Life   3
2. Twig's Favorite Animal   6
3. Angry at a Loved One? Look in the Mirror   9
4. A Decent Lawyer, Lover, and Man   12
5. One Way to Guarantee a Date   15
6. When Grown-ups Don't Grow Up   18
7. Mothering—A Crash Course for Fathers   21
8. The Richest Man in the World   24
9. Our Beliefs Can Be Our Legacy   27
10. The Eight Wonders of the World   30

II. DECIDING TO DECIDE

11. Acting on Sixty-Percent Convictions   35
12. All-or-Nothing Choices   38
13. The Liberation of Punxsutawney Phyllis   41
14. The Tyranny of the Tube   44
15. The Price of Self-Pity   47
16. The Great Burden of Keeping a Secret   50
17. A Lion's Lament   53
18. Live Free or Die?   56

19. Expensive Thrills   59
20. Betrayed by Loyalty   62

III. CASES OF MISTAKEN IDENTITY

21. Our Many Names and Numbers   67
22. Feeling Guilty When You're Not   70
23. The Wisdom of Inflatable Owls   73
24. Let Us Now Praise the Pigeons of the World   76
25. Advice from the Most Ignorant of Men   79
26. Confidence and Compliments   82
27. Shying from One Theory to the Next   85
28. The (Im)perfect Primer   88
29. To Forgive Is Divine—and Human   91

IV. A HALF-FULL CUP

30. Everyday Miracles   97
31. Talking to Cabbies Isn't Always Taxing   100
32. A Story Too Good to Be True   103
33. The Inspiring Effect of Praising Others   106
34. Insecurity Issues   109
35. "Are You Okay?"   112
36. When Opposites Attract   115
37. Saying No Can Be the Best Yes in Life   118
38. Turning Down Booze with a Smile   121
39. Is Happiness in the Cards?   124
40. Choosing to Be Happy   127
41. Crying in Our Cups   130

V. THE AVAILING STRUGGLE

42. Moments of Awakening   135
43. Confessions of a Repentant Racist   138

44. Meditation upon the Death of a Child   141
45. Bringing Yourself as a Gift   144
46. Kindness Doesn't Kill   147
47. Strong Hearts and Strong Shoulders   150
48. Snatching a Victory in the Final Moments   153
49. Do You Want to See? Then Turn Out the Lights   156
50. Learning God's Yes   159

All our life is a miracle. Ourselves are the greatest wonder of all
. . . I can believe a miracle because I can raise my own arm. I can
believe a miracle because I can remember. I can believe it because I
can speak and be understood by you. I can believe in a manifestation
of power beyond my own, because I am such a manifestation. . . . There
is not a minute in the twenty-four hours that is not filled with miracles.

—RALPH WALDO EMERSON

People talk about Bible miracles because there is no miracle in their
lives. Cease to gnaw that crust. There is ripe fruit over your head.

—HENRY DAVID THOREAU

Preface

For some odd reason, which I cannot begin to understand, none of the stories in this book has anything to do with baseball. Yet, almost every one of them is mirrored in a miracle that took place a decade ago during the fifth inning of an otherwise ordinary baseball game.

Since stories from life hinge upon the peculiar histories of their protagonists, a little background. My wife, Amy, and I got married in 1970. I was twenty-one, she was nineteen. Children of the sixties, we wanted to spend a little quality time together before the world came to an end.

For our wedding ceremony, Amy and I wrote our own vows —more on the order of a manifesto—declaring our pacifism and my personally convenient but nonetheless impassioned refusal to bear arms. That very month in the U.S. Senate, my father, Frank Church, was valiantly championing the Cooper-Church amendment, a law that would end our illegal bombing of Cambodia. I took no thought whatsoever of the effect our personal pronouncements might have on his efforts for peace.

He was better about this than my mother. When we proposed distributing printed copies of our vows to the guests, she, quite prudently, put her foot down. But one guest, a reporter, took extensive notes anyway, and the following week my father had to fend off questions concerning his family's quotient of patriotism.

Clearly, getting married didn't mean I had finally grown up. This only began in earnest nine years later. Which brings us to the ball game. Amy and I were sitting in the bleachers at Fenway Park in Boston. As one indication of the fact that I still had a lot of growing to do, my birthday gift to Amy on her twenty-seventh birthday was two tickets to a Red Sox game. What a generous, sacrificial act this was!

Not only that, but, the night before, she had left her contact lenses in too long. When she woke up she couldn't see. We rushed to the local emergency room, where the doctor anesthetized her eyes and put two patches on them. Not wanting to deprive Amy of her present, I took her to the ball park anyway.

So there we were, my blind date, seven months pregnant, and her ever-thoughtful husband, sitting in Fenway Park and watching, as it were, a baseball game. Sitting right in front of us were a man and his son. The boy was about ten, his father just a little older than me. The man put his arm around his son's shoulders, and all of a sudden it struck me, the real force and power of it struck me. I too was about to become a father. That very moment I stepped up one rung on the ladder of mortality. I was pushed up, really, by someone newly perched on the ladder behind me.

As I've reflected upon this moment—and it truly was an awakening—my understanding has deepened. Growing up, or knowing that I had better start soon, had less to do with impending parenthood than it did with being ready to give up some of my vaunted independence. It was a tough call. Imagine the luxury of being twenty-nine years old, in school all your life publishing an occasional world-shattering article, debating great ideas, being supported by your wife.

Freedom is wonderful. I cherished mine, and some of the

stories I include here attest to the fact that I still do. But today, I find freedom meaningful only when invested in something beyond my own piggy bank of personal pleasure. Becoming a father went a long way toward prompting me to barter some of my precious freedom for responsibility.

Responsibility has its problems too, of course. Today, at least half of the things I do I don't want to do. I don't want to take my children to school or pick them up afterward. I don't want to go to parents' nights or birthday parties. And I'd far rather cook dinner for people whose tastes run to something more exotic than macaroni and cheese. But I do these things. They're probably even good for me. And there are immediate payoffs: Not only do I get to put my arms around my son's shoulders, but I have someone to take to ball games who really wants to go.

That moment in the ball park ten years ago is what these stories from life are all about—little epiphanies, moments of awakening, everyday miracles. The privilege of writing them was presented to me by Tom Stites, then editor of the Tempo section of the *Chicago Tribune*. He took a considerable risk: publishing the thoughts of a clergyman (who wasn't either running for president or involved in a juicy scandal) in a respectable paper. I thank him for it, and the people of Chicago, too, especially those of you who have written spirit-boosting letters. Though I root for the Mets every time they play the Cubs, I still feel like an honorary citizen of one of the greatest cities in the world.

Another joy comes from working with two editors who have been unfailingly kind to me, Simon Michael Bessie, publisher of Cornelia & Michael Bessie books at Harper & Row, who gently midwifed my first book, *Father & Son,* into being, and Clayton

Carlson, publisher of Harper & Row, San Francisco, who published my trilogy, A *Humane Comedy*, three little books on hell, heaven, and purgatory.

I dedicate this one to my children, who—just like yours, if you happen to be blessed with children—are interchangeably the most wonderful and difficult children in the world. Speaking of everyday miracles, as Sophia Lyons Fahs once said, "Every night a child is born is a holy night."

I

FAMILY TIES

1

A Brush with Death—and Life

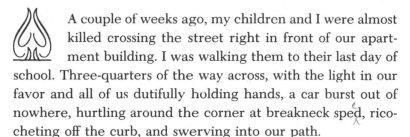 A couple of weeks ago, my children and I were almost killed crossing the street right in front of our apartment building. I was walking them to their last day of school. Three-quarters of the way across, with the light in our favor and all of us dutifully holding hands, a car burst out of nowhere, hurtling around the corner at breakneck sped, ricocheting off the curb, and swerving into our path.

I saw the driver clearly. We were so close we could have kissed. She was a beautiful woman with wild eyes. Missing us by inches, her car skidded, fishtailed back into control, and disappeared. I could barely breathe, my knees buckling, my heart beating like a pile driver. In stark contrast, my kids just laughed, romping blithely down the sidewalk, jumping from tree to tree as they always do, trying to touch the leaves.

Deeply shaken, not knowing what to think or say, I did the obvious thing. I got angry. Not at the driver, of course. She was gone. I vented my anger at the children. I decided to teach them a lesson they obviously had failed to learn from the experience.

"Never, never let your guard down when you're crossing the street. Did you see that car? It almost hit us. It really did. We could have been killed."

"Come off it, Dad," my eight-year-old son replied nonchalantly, jumping a second time at a branch that had eluded him.

By this time my six-year-old daughter was skipping around the next corner and was almost out of sight.

That did it. I exploded. If they remember anything about our somber walk to school that morning, it is that their father sometimes, with the slightest provocation, lapses into fits of wild irrationality. And they were right. Neither of them was doing anything wrong. They were holding my hands, walking with the signal. I had no lesson to teach them.

Only this, perhaps: Our lives are beset with trapdoors. Whenever the ground seems most secure, someone out there has his hand on the lever. A massive coronary, an embolism, a drunk driver, a strung-out addict drawing a pound of flesh for an ounce of crack. When the trapdoor springs, we haven't time for regrets or second chances, for anger or recrimination. It just happens. Swoosh. No good-byes.

I try to teach my children about life's dangers. We all do. Look both ways. Wear white after dark. Don't take candy from strangers. We answer their questions and dearly wish they'd ask us more. But put a mad driver behind the wheel and our lessons mean nothing.

Trapdoors have one saving grace: They add to our appreciation for life, even as they threaten to extinguish it. That very afternoon, walking my son and daughter home from school, they looked different to me, more vulnerable and precious. As we talked about their day at school and our summer plans, I loved them desperately.

It reminded me of something that I keep forgetting: Life is not a given, but a priceless gift. One day something will steal it from us, a seizure in the night or a driver in the morning, but that doesn't diminish its value. On the contrary, fragility and impermanence ensure life's preciousness. We can truly love only that which one day we must lose. It took a trapdoor trembling beneath my feet, and a crazed woman casting the shadow of death across my family's path, to awaken me once again to the wonder of life and the blessings of love.

But that's the way it is. Often, the most precious gifts come wrapped in odd packages. So odd, in fact, that if given a choice, almost certainly we would choose the wrong one. The one in fancy paper and topped with a bow. Never the one in brown paper wrapping tied with a string.

They didn't know it, but my kids had the right idea. We had just escaped from a brush with death. Why didn't I think to jump and touch the leaves?

Twig's Favorite Animal

 Three years ago today, purely by accident, my son and I got Abraham Lincoln's birthday right. We rediscovered freedom. At the zoo.

Things began poorly. Upon our entering through the wrong gate and wandering in a blinding snowstorm for ten minutes without seeing a single animal, my first thought was that anyone venturing willingly into a zoo in February deserved no sympathy. Finally, we spotted a bison. Given the circumstances, this was encouraging.

"Son," I said, with dutiful enthusiasm, "did you know that millions of buffalo once ranged freely in the Great Plains?"

"Hurry up, Daddy," he replied. "I'm really cold."

We trudged ahead toward a cluster of buildings, entering the nearest, an airplane hangar stocked with mangy elephants, submerged hippos, and the odd rhinoceros. However unpleasant—ripe and clammy—at least it was occupied by animals. All the buildings were. Sensibly, any animal given the option chose to remain inside. But where were the people? We wandered for nearly half an hour before encountering another human being.

Zoos without people are unutterably strange places, yet most of the animals didn't seem to mind. Only the monkeys. When we arrived at the monkey house, all was still. But as we strolled by the cages, the monkeys came to life. Hallelujah, finally an audience.

6

They jumped through tires. They swung on ropes. They hung upside down by their feet on the front of their cages. This was fun for a while but ultimately boring, so Twig and I headed for the cafeteria. All the people visiting the zoo that day were there. It was like a cageful of human beings.

"I wish it were summer," Twig said.

As we picked at our hamburgers in search of meat, I remembered how as a child I would long for the coming of summer. By February, the very thought of it was almost unbearably sweet. Summer meant freedom. Freedom from school. Freedom from indoors. Even freedom from my parents for a few choice weeks.

But then summer arrived. I can remember magic moments from the summers of my youth, but I also recall long stretches of boredom, as my best friend Jimmy Bruce and I sat together on the steps of my house in Boise almost any sultry, midsummer's day.

"Do you want to play baseball?"

"Nah, I'm tired of playing baseball."

"So am I." Long pause. "We could play soldiers, but we did that yesterday."

"How about Monopoly?"

"It takes too long."

And so we sat, plumped up in the very lap of summer, bored to tears. Nothing to do, no responsibilities, free as birds but nowhere to fly. Two little boys sighing on the stoop, budding existentialists weighted down by the burden of time on their hands and the liberty to do with it what they would. We could have done anything we wanted, but couldn't think of anything to do.

And then we grew up. Big boys now, still tempted to act only on our desires, go only where we wanted to go, and give only what we wished to give, we exchanged our stoop for a drink and a couch. We still called it freedom, but most of the time we were simply building cages for ourselves, places where we would be safe from real and imagined storms. Nothing ventured, nothing lost.

"What is your favorite animal so far?" I asked my son as we sat together finishing our lunch.

He pointed out the window at a black squirrel perched on the roof of the building next door. For a while she watched us with acute interest, then leaped gracefully into a tree and disappeared. In its way, the squirrel was more interesting even than the monkeys. Perhaps it's because she was free.

Twig tugged at my arm. "Come on, Dad, let's go outside."

And so we did. We walked, and ran, and played in the snow until we couldn't feel our toes.

3

Angry at a Loved One?
Look in the Mirror

My dentist is one of the nicest people I know, although I never want to see her again. At least not in her office. Perhaps because she is a woman I feel obliged to act courageous in the dental chair—a good bluff while it lasts, which isn't long. When she puts on her mask and gloves and picks up something sharp, I fold like an empty hand.

The last time I visited her, I tried to postpone the inevitable by asking about her fish. This was a mistake. The colorful little fish in the bowl on her counter turns out to be a Siamese fighting fish. With the possible exceptions of the piranha, barracuda, and great white shark, no fish is more macho than this little monster.

"Look," my dentist said, holding up a small mirror to the side of the bowl. When the Siamese fighting fish saw its reflection, instantly it turned ferocious and gorgeous, flaring its fins into full fighting regalia and fiercely attacking its apparent adversary. Sorry I asked.

My dentist clearly admired this fish, and I was afraid I knew why. Believe me, in the presence of a woman who relishes such things, the imminent prospect of displaying less courage than a fish is humbling.

Whenever I am frightened, I try to talk my way out of it. That is another problem with dentists. They chatter along, presumably to help one relax, but being muzzled, one can't do anything but grunt in response. On this occasion some of my darker thoughts were allayed when my dentist began ruminating upon the relationship between the fighting fish's behavior and human nature. To my surprise, her observations had nothing to do with courage, fierceness, or the pageantry of battle. Instead her thoughts turned to the ways in which we transfer our anger against ourselves to others.

"It happens with my mother," she said. "When I see myself in my mother—some irritating affectation or her tendency to rationalize—I get angry, not at myself but at her. That fish, too, sees something he doesn't like in the glass and attacks. But what he really sees is himself."

I thought back to when I was in college. My friends and I spent an enormous amount of time drinking beer and playing poker. Every time I got fed up with myself, I expressed anger at them for wasting their lives. I preached on this subject until they anointed me "Moral Man." Once I even managed to talk myself into boycotting their decadent company for a whole week, but mostly I saved my moral outrage for the daylight hours, joining them in the evening for "a game or two" that stretched on through the night.

The reason family blood so often curdles is that we tend to resemble certain of our relatives in temperament and character; they are reminders of who we really are. I remember one late-night conversation at college, when each of us took turns indicting our parents for how we had turned out. One recurring theme was that we had inherited their worst characteristics but, unlike them, knew full well how debilitating these were.

One of my friends laughed. "You know, I've always felt sorry for myself because I was an orphan, but listening to you guys, I'm not so sure I wasn't the lucky one."

ing an unrespectable paper to catch up on the latest gossip. But sometimes the conversation at a nearby table is so fascinating I can't help but listen in. Take the couple who shoehorned themselves into the table next to mine and good-naturedly remarked how "cozy" it was. After they ordered, the man asked his wife, "If you had to describe your husband in a single word, what would it be?" *Good question,* I thought. *Let's see, my wife is amiable, conscientious, thoughtful, understanding, forgiving. But one word? Which would I choose?*

"Decent," she replied. "You're a decent lawyer, a decent provider, a decent lover. But above all, you're a decent man."

How wonderfully the word shifts its meaning from those first three statements to the fourth. She was telling her husband, with the ego-deflating prerogative that belongs to every spouse, that he was only a fair lawyer, a passable provider, and no great shakes as a lover, while at the same time assuring him that none of this really mattered, because in her eyes he was truly a good man.

The world is littered with brilliant lawyers, but we still put a premium on their talent. Many people make far more money than they know what to do with, but having too much money will never go out of fashion. And what self-respecting man would welcome being dismissed by his wife as being unexceptional in bed? Yet, this woman had just given her husband the highest compliment that could be contained in a single word. *Decent.*

Decent has a third meaning too, as in the Legion of Decency, which in the fifties banded together under a religious banner on a moralistic crusade to clean up the movies. Here the word means *chaste, clean, modest, unsullied, pure.* But that's not what she meant at all. Her husband might well have been the sort of fellow who falls asleep while reading *The Joy of Sex* while lying next to her in bed, but in calling him a decent man, she wasn't describing a prude or a goody-two-shoes, just a good, honest person. He couldn't have been more pleased.

When I returned home that afternoon, I considered asking my wife the same question but quickly thought better of it. Like a guest on Groucho Marx's old TV show, I could imagine waiting fruitlessly for that silly duck to fall from the sky with the magic word *decent* in its bill.

I'm not that rash a gambler, especially with my ego on the line. As for the adjectives my wife might conjure up, while I waited for the magic word to appear, I'd rather not speculate. Besides, after two martinis on a free afternoon, I couldn't expect her to welcome my frivolous interruption of her work and had reasonable fears that this might slant her list accordingly.

So, acting in character, I held my tongue. After all, it was the only decent thing to do.

5

One Way to Guarantee a Date

Marriage is far from being a perfect institution. Yet, among its advantages are little things we married folks tend to take for granted. For instance, marriage rescues awkward people—which means most of us—from the terrors of dating.

I discovered this anew when flipping through the pages of my high-school yearbook for the first time in years. My strongest-remembered emotion was embarrassment. The names and faces, long since forgotten, of girls I once lacked the courage to ask out; untold hours spent staring at the phone; and, then, finally calling, only to hang up after two rings or when their fathers answered: In high school, I was a pillar of inadequacy.

Once, I even resorted to clipping out a picture of some model from *Newsweek* magazine and putting her in my wallet, so that I would have a girlfriend should the need arise. Unfortunately, not only did the words on the other side of the page bleed through, but this person was apparently known by everyone but me. When I tested her out on someone I had hopes of impressing, she said, "'That's Jean Shrimpton," and mortified me further by telling all her friends.

Perversely intrigued by the rekindled bathos of these memories, I traced my embarrassment all the way back to my first, telling encounter with the opposite sex. I was only thirteen. If you have ever wondered why thirteen is considered an

15

unlucky number, think back for a moment to when you were thirteen. If we could only skip a year the way hotels skip a floor, thirteen would win hands down.

The month I turned thirteen, I fell in love with a girl named Jackie Stump. I never spoke to her, of course, but apparently my affections were transparent to the well-trained eye. My seventh-grade geography teacher, who should have been dismissed for torture, wrote on the board one day just before we entered class, "Wherever there's a Forrest, there's a Stump." I could have died.

In desperation, I concocted a plan. To prove him wrong, all I had to do was "go steady" with someone else. After a careful analysis of the available prospects, I chose Donna, a girl who couldn't possibly turn me down.

Only one obstacle remained. The problem of the ring. Being in a great hurry, and not eager to lay out a lot of money, I rummaged around in our basement and found an old jewelry box of my mother's. In this trove of tarnished treasure, I uncovered dozens of pins, pendants, and bracelets, but not a single ring.

Undaunted, I fixed upon a heavy pair of silver earrings that had a ringlike look about them. I would make a ring for Donna. This wasn't easy, by the way. The earring was slightly bulky, even baroque in appearance, a bit off shape—for a ring, that is —and open at the bottom. I attacked it with a hammer.

Fortunately, earrings come in pairs, so I had a spare to work with. This time, employing needle-nosed pliers, I deftly broke off the little clamp that once held Donna's ring to my mother's ear, and closed, as best I could, the aperture. Believe me, this was not a normal, everyday "friendship" ring, but a special, modern, new kind of ring, a tad large perhaps, but that didn't matter. One wore such things on a chain around one's neck. And my mother had lots of old chains.

Flushed with excitement, the next morning I proposed to Donna outside geography class. She treated me more kindly than I deserved, and didn't return my ring until the next morning. "It would probably be better for all concerned," she said, "if you gave the broken earring back to your mother, who might be able to fix it."

Strangely enough, these memories contain their own solace, a simple reminder that it's been almost twenty years now since I've had to suffer the embarrassment of trying to win the affections of any woman other than my wife. It's the sort of thing that gives marriage a good name.

Not that Amy and I go on dates as often as perhaps we should, but whenever I ask, I don't have to worry. She already has my ring. And almost never turns me down.

6

When Grown-ups Don't Grow Up

I met a brand-new human being recently, the week-old son of one of my parishioners. Everything he did was fascinating. He opened his eyes. He made strange and wonderful noises. He clutched my finger in one of his perfect little hands and wouldn't let go. I was thrilled.

I must confess, it doesn't always thrill me when I hold my nine-year-old son's hand, although it should. What it usually means is that we are late for school and he isn't walking fast enough. And I'm not exactly swept away, just relieved, when he opens his eyes in the morning. After all, if you shake a sleeping child vigorously enough, he's bound to open his eyes eventually.

Until recently Twig was not a morning person. When he finally managed to blink into consciousness, his eyes had a daggerlike quality. He squinted at his father, then made a strange but hardly wonderful noise, expressive of profound disgust. For the next hour, as the appointed representatives of morning, his mother and I daily bore the brunt of Twig's resistance against dressing, breakfast, toothbrushing, his sister, school, and life.

Last year we discovered that Twig, a bright and thoughtful child, has a learning disability. He has trouble doing some things that come easily to others. But he grows every day, some days more than other children, because he overcomes difficulties, which make his triumphs all the more impressive.

As he grows up, much of my pleasure is selfish. He has

18

reached that wonderful age when all of a sudden he knows the names and averages of my favorite ballplayers. When we watch the news together, he offers telling commentary. And when he laughs, which is increasingly often, he lights up the room.

How delightful to watch children grow. Before we become bored with one miracle, they perform a new one. I was still taking joy in my son's first words when he ventured his first step. Then, before I lost interest in watching him walk, he began to string words together into sentences, and then draw pictures, and write words and sentences and read them to me. Had I known how hard this was for him, I would have appreciated it even more.

But what about the rest of us? What happens when we grow up, when being forty is not so different from being fifty? If being grown up means we stop growing—ideas set, habits ingrained —then other people, even our spouses and friends, may ever so slowly but quite understandably begin to lose interest. Grown-ups have a hard time growing up. More often than not we grow down. Many of the most accomplished adolescents I know are fifty-year-old men.

We don't have to grow down, of course. My wife just started a new, challenging job, and it's amazing how much she has changed. I loved her before, but I didn't know how much. In her new job, Amy is a new woman, more engaging, more alive. Sometimes as I drift off to sleep, the last sounds I hear are her tapping at her computer. And often when I wake up she already has showered and dressed, and is ready for the day. Other important things, which she would kill me for mentioning, have changed as well.

The point is, across the board, with her life so much more exciting, she exudes excitement. She's even become more tolerant of my idiosyncrasies, which one day I may or may not grow out of. After all, she has less time to bother herself with them.

I, strangely, am less tolerant of myself. I know now why some men don't want their wives to continue growing. No real surprise here. It puts the pressure on us to grow as well.

My son loves his new school, a wonderful school for learning-disabled children. Every day he amazes me by how much he is learning and growing. Today I was the last one in our family to get up. "Come on, Dad," my son said, prodding me. "Mommy and Nina have already had breakfast, and if you don't hurry, I'm going to be late for school."

Okay, kid. I guess it's about time your old dad started growing up.

7

Mothering—A Crash Course for Fathers

This week I celebrate the third anniversary of my attempt at motherhood. I am a fool to bring this up. No unregenerate male should. Yet among my experiences, my limited stint as a mother is among the most telling.

I used to know what being a mother, or full-time father, was all about. Having spent the better part of one day a week as primary care-giver to my children, I thought I was acquainted with the basics. I was wrong.

This was brought home with chastening effect when my wife, Amy, contracted pneumonia. She fell ill when we were on a family vacation. At first, my sacrifice was limited to playing with our children on the beach, a sandy job, but someone had to do it. When we returned to New York and discovered the serious nature of her illness, things abruptly changed. I was humbled by reality.

Because our home was filled with dust from recent construction, the doctor banished Amy to a luxurious convalescence with close friends. Let me tell you about my three weeks with the children. I did quite well, for about two days. By the middle of the first week, my then three-year-old daughter, Nina, and five-year-old son, Twig, had taken charge. From that point on,

21

together we embarked upon what I since have come to regard as an experiment in living.

Because of renovations, our apartment was torn up. There was no kitchen, and most of the rest of the apartment was covered in oilcloth. Accordingly, the three of us lived in two back rooms. Our circumstances, coupled with my inadequacy as a parent, brought out Nina and Twig's latent talent for absolute, if subtle, self-aggrandizement. As I tried to perform my duty, they seized every opportunity to fulfill all manner of hitherto undreamed of aspirations. Falling asleep at midnight in front of the television set. Trashing their parents' bedroom. Going for days without a bath. Having Cheerios for dinner. That sort of thing.

School was not yet in session, so they tagged along with me to work, each with a Tupperware container of dry Cheerios. (Remember, we had no refrigerator, so milk was out of the question.) They proceeded to take over the church offices, attending wedding conferences, terrorizing the staff, sleeping on my office sofa to make up for losses hard-won the night before. Actually, they were really quite good. That is to say, normal, rotten, wonderful kids. Which is one reason single or even primary parenting is so difficult. It's not the things that go wrong that get to you, but the endless repetition and accumulation of everyday things.

At first, the whole business reminded me of the myth of Sisyphus. Every day you roll this stone of yours up to the top of the mountain. Then, just when you reach the top, ready for a well-deserved rest, you lose your grip. Before you can do anything about it, your stone is screaming down the mountain, bouncing to the bottom once again. It doesn't matter how tired you are or how many other things you have to do. You pick your body up, and down you go again. You love your stone, of course.

Besides, it doesn't know any better than to roll down to the bottom of the mountain every time you get it to the top.

I have observed that eventually one gets rather skilled at this. To be fair to myself, three weeks was not a sufficient test. But it was long enough for me to discover that rearing children is actually the opposite of the myth of Sisyphus. Far from being a parable of futility, parental rock and roll is charged with meaning, every single beat. Sometimes you can't miss it. Things like "You're the best daddy in the whole wide world" go a long way toward reminding us that no burden is more precious than those we shoulder when nurturing our children.

So the next time someone asks you what you do, go ahead and tell them that you're just a lawyer or just a banker. But if blessed with the burden of children, never let anyone catch you saying that you're just a housewife or mother or father. After all, you are in charge of the creation.

8

The Richest Man in the World

My grandfather was the richest man in the world. I know this because whenever I visited his home, he would slip me a five-dollar bill. "Spend it on anything you want," he'd say, "but don't tell your parents."

I remember Chase Clark as a short man with twinkling eyes and a shock of white hair. When he was two, his family moved to Idaho from Indiana. Sixty years later the people of Idaho elected him governor. But that isn't what made him special. A self-educated lawyer who specialized in everything from shotgun weddings to moonshine, he bought all his clients new boots so that if they went to jail they wouldn't catch cold.

My grandparents lost one child, but when my grandmother got pregnant again, Chase Clark, concerned about her health, closed his law practice, and they moved to Salt Lake City. For the next six months, they waited together for my mother to be born. His practice didn't suffer. Neither did his pocketbook. Having accepted land in lieu of fees, he owned tens of thousands of acres, many of them in the area that is now Sun Valley. At the time of the first great Wall Street crash, Chase Clark was a member of the board of the largest bank in the area. The bank folded as a casualty of the Depression. Keeping only his ranch, he sold all his land at dirt prices, personally making good on every small investor's holding.

In 1940 he was elected governor but was defeated for re-election in 1942. Early that year, a Catholic priest went to him pleading for action to redress the growing problem of overcrowding at the state penitentiary. There were nearly three times as many prisoners as the penitentiary was built to hold. Murderers were sharing cells with pickpockets. Within three months of election day, my grandfather pardoned more than one hundred prisoners. Only two ever returned behind bars—several showed up for his funeral in 1966—but the issue for which his opponent had been praying presented itself. Having been convinced that it was no longer safe to walk the streets at night, the voters turned against Chase Clark, and he lost by two hundred votes.

My grandfather died when I was in my first year at college. But it wasn't until much later that my parents told me something about him which truly startled me. The richest man in the world left almost nothing in his will. At first even my parents couldn't understand this. But then they looked through his books. For years, at the end of every month, he cleaned out his accounts: fifty dollars here, twenty dollars there. Everything he didn't need for food or mortgage payments he gave away to good causes and derelict relatives.

Now I know why—to my delight as a child—his desk drawers were chock-full of trinkets. Some boys club in Omaha would send him a plastic American flag lapel pin, and he would respond with a check. And every Christmas morning, as each of us took turns unwrapping his lavish gifts and then telling him he shouldn't have gone overboard the way he did, he'd simply reply, "You can't take it with you."

I had a poor relative too. The only time she ever took us all out to dinner, she left her purse at home. Intelligent and strong, she lived simply in a tiny duplex apartment. When I graduated from high school she gave me a fifty-dollar savings bond. That was twenty years ago, which means I can finally cash it in for full face value. If only I knew where it was. But I didn't mind. She was poor, and anyway, my rich grandfather gave me a car when I graduated. Who could ask for more?

What I didn't know is that over the years my poor relative had shrewdly amassed a small fortune. She spent her life roosting on a golden egg, which hatched when she died.

So I had it wrong when I was a little boy. But only partly wrong, for in the only way it matters, my grandfather far surpassed her in riches. After all, he knew that our true wealth is measured not by what we leave behind but by what we can afford to give away before we go.

9

Our Beliefs Can Be Our Legacy

More than a century ago, my great-great-grandfather, a Mormon bishop who traveled west with Brigham Young and then settled in Idaho, wrote his will. I found it in a family album, on lined pages in a careful, cursive hand. The first thing I noticed was that this will had nothing to do with the distribution of funds or property. It was wholly devoted to matters of moral, civic, and religious concern.

In many ways my grandfather's will resembled the "ethical wills" of thirteenth- and fourteenth-century Jews: "Study the Scriptures, obey your teachers, keep the Sabbath, do not stray from the Commandments, live a studious, upright and pure life, or you will forgo my parental blessing." Knowing my own children, I'm afraid I couldn't get away with this. Even if I were dead. Still, the idea of an ethical will fascinates me.

Can you think of any more challenging exercise than setting down on paper those things you hold most dear, things you would wish your own children or other loved ones to weigh and measure in the living and dying of their own precious days? Ideally, we shouldn't have to write such things down. As Thomas Jefferson said, "It is in our lives, and not our words, that our religion must be read." But sometimes our lives need a little help.

Even as I write this, from my window I see that the rush-hour traffic has slowed to near-standstill. Soon, after a good deal of effort, families such as mine will be gathering for dinner. Parents will oversee baths and toothbrushing and once again discover whether, by some miracle, books will be read and the children tucked in at an hour roughly proximate to their appointed bedtime. But I promise you one thing: In my household, the odds are long against our having a deep or telling conversation with our children tonight. Daddy is tired. Mommy is tired. And we know that our children have their own agenda: to avoid baths and postpone bedtime as long as possible.

It's not that my wife and I never get down to serious business. Goodness knows, our children have provoked many heart-to-heart chats. Out of the blue, one will ask us something unexpected about God, death, or "being good." When this happens, we do our best, half the time learning as much from their off-the-wall observations as they do from our off-the-cuff responses. The problem is, we could go on like this forever. Yet, as our own parents so often remind us, how quickly the time passes. Before we know it our children will be grown. Which leads me back to my great-great-grandfather and his ethical will.

Is it useful, or even possible, to attempt such a thing today? The idea may be daunting, but the discipline of taking time to reflect on the things we have learned is potentially worth more than many equally unnatural drills, such as jogging, that are in vogue today.

To be sure, whether we record our values for posterity or not, we cannot help but pass them on to our children. They may reject them or expose them as fraudulent, but the things we hold most dear, the nature of our priorities and the limits we impose upon our own behavior, are by far the most enduring part of our legacy. But not the only part. Think about our wills. Wills, too, are a reflection of our values and priorities. When we finally get around to writing our wills, we tend to agonize, weighing the proper distribution of money, property, and things.

Even as a legal will accounts for our possessions, by drawing up an ethical will we would be challenged to weigh and measure our most cherished legacy, the truth by which we live. What are we living for? And what would we die for? How would we rank faith, love, friendship, knowledge, duty, money, success, and kindness, knowing that often they conflict with one another? What is the purpose of life? And of death?

I wonder. Did my great-great-grandfather really write that ethical will only for his children, or did he also write it for himself?

10

The Eight Wonders of the World

 A parishioner of mine took his nine-year-old son camping this summer. My memory of camping is trout for breakfast—you catch it, you eat it—but this guy pulled out all the stops. He introduced his son to the grandeur of creation, California's rugged mountainous majesty.

As he regaled me with details of their adventure, I felt a twinge of jealousy, but only a twinge. After all, if diehard high-rise dwellers had backyards, or even liked them very much, even I might spring for a tent and take my nine-year-old son camping. Just imagine: the two of us in sleeping bags on a concrete balcony gazing out at the stars (all three of them), with me pointing out that the unflickering one is not a star at all but the planet Venus. But I know better. In places like New York and Chicago, even planets flicker through the shimmering haze of a sky lit by monuments and polluted by machines.

This other kid's father is an architect. Judging from his buildings, the mountains and stars inspire him. Not that I hold him responsible for the destruction of the starlit sky, but he does design some of those magnificent towers that supplant nature, domineering the heavens with their own brilliant luminosity. Last summer he and his son stood gazing out upon a different sky, the clouds catching fire as the sun dipped through the horizon, yielding to pastel ribbons, then gently darkening the heavens until, one by one, the stars came out.

"This is the eighth wonder of the world," the man said to his son.

"What are the other seven?" asked the boy.

Well, can you name the Seven Wonders of the World, a group of remarkable creations of ancient times? Off the top of my head, I conjured up three: the Egyptian pyramids, the Hanging Gardens of Babylon, and the Colossus of Rhodes. Not bad. But just in case one of my children should ask the same question on some future camping expedition, I took out a little insurance, looking up the other four in my encyclopedia. Here they are: the tomb of Mausolus at Halicarnassus; the temple of Artemis at Ephesus; the statue of Zeus by Phidias at Olympia; and the Pharos (or lighthouse) of Alexandria.

Of course.

When it came to the Seven Wonders of the World, my friend the architect had a built-in advantage: Architects designed six of them. But he didn't tell this story to boast of his craft. Quite the opposite.

Yes, he answered his son's question, describing each of these marvels in considerable detail. Then the two of them stood silently together, until the sky wound itself into a riot of stars. Minutes passed. The man felt proud. But not nearly so proud as he soon would feel.

"Dad?"

"Yes, son?"

"Those things you told me about. They aren't the real seven wonders of the world."

"What do you mean, son?"

"The first wonder of the world is a woman having a baby. Don't you think so, Dad? The second is being able to see. Then comes being able to talk and walk. That's four. Hearing makes five. Then either touch or smell, maybe both."

Looking upon the creation with new eyes, his father said, "How about love?"

"Love," his son repeated. "That's the eighth wonder of the world."

Among other things, this story reminded me that I have no excuse for not taking my son camping. I don't really spend all summer in the city. My family and I vacation in California, but since I survive in California by pretending it's New York, the idea simply never occurred to me. Even though the lesson of my friend's story has more to do with children than with camping, maybe I will try out the mountains next summer. Who knows. Standing by my children's side and gazing at the universe, I might even learn something.

II

DECIDING TO DECIDE

11

Acting on Sixty-Percent Convictions

 A young man came to me for counseling. For a number of years he had been living with a woman. She wanted to get married, but he wasn't convinced. He didn't know if he was good enough for her and wasn't sure she was the right woman for him. For months he had been agonizing, going back and forth, paralyzed, unable to decide. Above all else, he was terribly worried about making the wrong decision, about doing the wrong thing. And so he did nothing at all. In many ways, he was a typical, late-twentieth-century, thirty-five-year-old, successful, unmarried man. That is to say, he was scared to death of commitment.

I met with him three times. We made no progress. He simply couldn't decide. Finally, after eight months, I began to get bored. Not wanting to have him follow me to the grave with his problem, I said this to him: "There are only four possibilities. You will either get married and be thankful, or get married and regret that you did, or not get married and be thankful, or not get married and regret that you didn't." The question was not whether he should get married; the question was whether he would be thankful, and the only way to find that out was to act. There was a long pause. He finally asked, "Well, what should I do?"

"Be thankful," I replied.

I told this story to my mother. She responded by saying she would remember never to send anyone to me for counseling.

Over the years I have developed the following somewhat simplistic but possibly useful approach to decision-making. Two elements are involved in every decision. The first is conviction: Do we know what we ought to do? The second is action: Are we going to do it? Put the two together, and the question becomes, What does it take for us to act?

Some people never act, no matter what. At an early age, they must have discovered how safe it was under the bed. Others are absolutely sure of themselves. They're the ones we have to watch out for, the one-hundred-percenters. (One hint: They have a penchant for religion and politics.) But what about the rest of us? Most of us have sixty-percent convictions. It's a reasonable quandary to have in this confounding world. But when it comes to taking a stand, sixty percent is sometimes not enough. Eager to act but unsure of ourselves, we are often paralyzed and cannot act at all. As in "Should I get married?" or "Should I do what I believe is right, even though it will complicate my life?"

What about abortion or capital punishment or the arms race or any of the great issues of our time? When pressed, many of us feel that the way we are leaning is correct, but still we are not one-hundred-percent sure, at least not sure enough or energetic enough to act on our sixty-percent convictions in such a way that others would have to stand up and take notice. And so we don't act. We don't write our representative or join a protest or commit our precious money. Not being one-hundred-percent sure, we don't risk committing ourselves.

There has to be a better way. What about acting on sixty-percent convictions and acting energetically—risking the effort, possible failure, and even embarrassment such actions entail on the prudent gambler's chance that we will make a small difference in the world or in a single human life, perhaps even our own?

Almost every important decision I have ever made has been based on sixty-percent convictions. Yet, often I don't act. Actions entail risk, and I am no more courageous than anyone else. But I do know that not to act is to act. It is to act on behalf of that which I don't believe in. Call it the forty-percent solution. We do more by inaction to foster the things we oppose than we do by our actions to nurture the things we support.

By the way, the young man did get married. In fact, he and his wife turned up on my doorstep just a few months ago. Both of them were radiant, but they had a problem. She was pregnant, and, given her age, their doctor was strongly urging amniocentesis to detect potential birth defects. She was frightened by the test and not at all sure that she would be willing to have an abortion regardless of how the test came out. He was just frightened.

I didn't have anything particularly helpful to say to them, other than to trust themselves again, act according to their consciences, and be prepared to make what in retrospect might possibly appear to be a mistaken decision.

This time, we met only once. The three of them are doing just fine.

12

All-or-Nothing Choices

It has been a curious week. Almost everyone I've talked to has been living on the cusp. It's an old astrological term, meaning halfway between one sign and another. Between cities, between jobs, between loves, balancing past and future on a decision that must be made.

I know what it means to live on the cusp. I was born on September 23. According to some astrologers this makes me a Virgo; according to others, a Libra. I am on the cusp, halfway between. Virgo: pure, rigid, disciplined, left-brained, "an impeccable life player." Libra: balanced but artistic, open, creative, right-brained, "the fool of justice, seeking all that is harmonious."

If astrology were the state religion, I wouldn't be on the cusp, I'd be on the rack. You know those daily forecasts that run in the paper. Next time you read one, try putting the Virgo and the Libra forecast together. If Virgo reads, "This is the day you've been waiting for; go for it, love, money, everything; don't miss a single opportunity to make a new connection," Libra is sure to say, "Take the day off; better yet, don't even get out of bed; you might break your leg on the way to the bathroom."

One advantage of living on the cusp is that I've never been tempted to take astrology all that seriously. Yet, the cusp metaphor is a good one. Balancing a plate of radically different choices is difficult but bracing. It reminds us how important our choices are. Also, that no matter what we choose, nothing good comes without risk, venture, and pain.

Pain gets a bad rap these days. We are living in the age of the pleasure principle. But remember, pain is our body's way of telling us that it's doing everything possible to help make us well again. The same thing goes for our soul. The pain of a bad conscience is what reminds us that we've done something wrong. Having a bad conscience doesn't mean you are a bad person. It means that you are a basically good person who has done something wrong and doesn't know what to do about it.

There are ways to short-circuit the conscience and cut off the pain. I might recommend Limbo. In old-time theology, Limbo was a special precinct of Hell, reserved for innocents. Translated into our daily lies, it is where basically good people are sent, not to freeze or burn, just to be forever without escape.

Limbo is not going out because you aren't sure you'll have a good time.

Limbo is not speaking out when injustice is done because you're afraid that no one will listen.

Limbo is holding out for the wheel of fate to spin in your direction.

Limbo is dropping out the moment that life gets difficult, when the going gets too interesting for you.

Limbo is for people who postpone decisions, who want to ensure that they'll never be wrong.

It's not that Limbo doesn't have its attractions. For one thing, there's little sharp pain in Limbo, only the dull throb of uncertainty, which we may elevate to the status of pain but which doesn't begin to compare with the honest pain of those who dare to act, knowing full well they may be wrong.

Not withstanding such advantages, when it comes to causes

you believe in, actions you are contemplating, or life decisions you face, you'd do well to throw caution to the wind, order up a future, pay generously for it, and tip imprudently. Half the time you will be wrong, but that's all right. Accept your mistakes as the price of admission for a life fully lived. In fact, daring to make mistakes is the only way to spring the gates of Limbo. It's also the best way I know to ensure that when the time comes for you to die, you will have lived in such a way that your life will prove to have been worth dying for.

13

The Liberation of Punxsutawney Phyllis

Late last January, on our way to school one morning, my then eight-year-old son made a curious pronouncement. He just had to watch the evening news on February 2. "Don't let me forget, Daddy. Please don't let me forget."

I must confess to a secret rush of pleasure. Just imagine: the two of us sitting down to watch the news together; he asking his father intelligent questions about current events and pro basketball; his father answering in a thoughtful yet age-appropriate manner, leading the boy gently toward an appreciation for the responsibilities of citizenship and the pleasure grown men get out of playing boy's games. Wouldn't it be grand.

"Sure, Twig," I nonchalantly replied. "I'll be happy to remind you. Perhaps we'll even watch the news together." We walked on hand in hand, each lost in his own reverie. As we entered the doors to his school, I couldn't help but ask, "Twig, tell me, what got you all fired up about watching the news on February 2?"

"Don't you know anything, Dad? That's the day we find out whether or not the groundhog saw his shadow."

So it was that I happened to be watching when the story broke, the biggest groundhog story of all time.

As you remember, when Punxsutawney Phil, the resident groundhog sage of Gobbler's Knob, Pennsylvania, returned to

his burrow having gone out to look for his shadow for the ump-
teenth time, his wife told him firmly that she'd had it. From now
on she would be the one to shoulder the burden of determining
whether or not spring was coming early.

Twig and I listened in shock as Punxsutawney Phyllis said,
"This is simply too important a matter to leave any longer to the
judgment of my dogmatically minded husband."

Many commentators have speculated on her motivations.
My guess is that she had long since dismissed the whole exercise
as a lot of hokum. Anything which gave her husband an official
pretext to come back into their hole and sleep for six more
weeks had to be a scam. She intended to get to the bottom of
it.

"Look at it this way," she said. "A shadow is a fact. Either
it's there or it's not. If it is there, the sun is shining; if not, the
day is cloudy. So what does my high-brow husband do with this
evidence? He looks out upon a single day and projects a six-
week outcome. Not only that, but his prediction flies in the face
of what he sees. Through some perverse twist of convoluted
logic, if the sun is shining, winter is far from over; if not, spring
is in the air.

"I'm not going to ruin my life anymore on the basis of one
day's experience," she continued, "especially when he draws
illogical conclusions from it. I can't count the number of times
the two of us have spent six ridiculous weeks walking through
the snow without coats on, or boarding ourselves up in our hole
while the sun, warm and wonderful, beat down upon the earth.
And all because my idiot husband believes in somebody else's
idiot theory."

Next week the world will be watching to see whether she
manages to hold to her guns. Most pundits, citing history and
nature, say the odds are against her. Remember, after having

seen his shadow last year, Punxsutawney Phil himself, just before tucking himself into bed for six more weeks of winter, issued a press release emphatically reasserting his intention to persevere. "This is man's work," he insisted. "Always has been, always will be." Many sympathized, including, surprisingly, some women. After all, nothing is more pathetic than a male with a crushed ego.

I told my daughter, Nina, about this. She seems to have the whole thing figured out. This year they'll both emerge from their hole and take a look. And if the sun is shining, both will go back inside.

"You mean she'll give in and follow his lead?"

"Of course not, Daddy! He'll go back to bed, and she'll unpack her spring clothing."

"And if it's raining, and they don't see their shadows?"

"Then she'll go inside," my daughter said, "and he'll get wet."

14

The Tyranny of the Tube

 If it were up to me, I'd never go out at night. I'm not afraid of the dark. I'm just lazy. Once I get home, my goal is to unplug myself. I mix a drink, curl into a comfortable chair, hope the phone doesn't ring, watch a baseball game, and drift off to sleep. Heaven.

Face it, for most of us, sex is not the greatest of life's temptations, or drugs, or even money. The greatest temptation is oblivion.

About a year ago the D'Arcy Masius Benton & Bowles advertising folks published a report titled "Fears and Fantasies of the American Consumer." Three-quarters of us evidently have daydreamed about saving someone's life and one in three about finding a cure for cancer. But when asked about our greatest pleasure in life, watching television tops the list. It turns out that we'd love to be good and live exciting lives, so long as we don't have to miss the latest miniseries.

We're especially good at dreaming. When asked about their "dream" job, men go in for adventure: professional athlete, test pilot, and race-car driver are three of the top five. The top fantasy vacation for men is to go on a safari. Women prefer a week of gambling in Monte Carlo. The report concludes that "while the dream is of Indiana Jones . . . the life is much more Walter Mitty. . . . In real life, it seems that the closest Americans

44

get to true adventure is watching 'Magnum, P.I.' from the living room couch. While nearly everyone bad-mouths television, it holds an absolutely central place in people's lives."

In a way, watching television is the midlife equivalent of "doing your own thing." In the sixties, my generation's rallying cry was "Turn on, tune in, and drop out." Apparently, today our dream is to turn on the TV, tune in our favorite channel, and drop out into oblivion. In both cases, the trouble with doing our own thing—those things we know will please us—is that over time we find fewer things pleasing, and even from them we get increasingly less pleasure. It's curious. We cloister ourselves in enclosed gardens with ever-higher walls. We burrow into our prisons quite happily until one day, too late, we realize we have forgotten where we put the key.

I am no exception. When I manage to stay home in the evening, I put my own life aside and become a world-class voyeur. Someone invented the CNN news just for me. If I stay up long enough, I can see the same story three times. There's only one problem: My better angel keeps provoking me to accept evening engagements.

Not that I can't wangle out of them: the committee meeting will go on without me, I say; no one will notice if I don't show up at some gala reception for yet another good cause; and I could see that play another night. Even so, for four nights running I have somehow managed to drag myself out of my comfortable chair, shave, change, and plunge back into the city, to my office for evening appointments, to a seminar, to deliver a lecture, to a friend's house for supper. And for four evenings straight I had a wonderful time.

I still hate going out. Probably always will. No matter how splendid I feel after seeing a great show, or after a successful meeting, or upon spending an evening with new acquaintances or old, inertia takes over and the feeling fades.

I have to go out again tonight. Part of me would die to retreat into my little shell and watch TV instead. But I won't. Not tonight, anyway. I've found that the only way to break the lock of my own prison is to keep on doing things I'd rather not do. It's the difference between growing up instead of simply growing old.

I'll skip the safari, and can promise you I'll never find a cure for cancer, but that's okay. By doing things I don't want to do, I may yet save a life—perhaps my own.

15

The Price of Self-Pity

Ever into self-improvement, I spent a few choice days this summer lying flat on my back, not on the beach but in bed. It's hardly my favorite form of character building, but temporary, complete debilitation does offer lessons in humility.

If you wish to take the cure but have only a little free time to devote to self-improvement, a crash course may be in order. Drawing on recent experience, let me recommend a few days of bed rest, preferably spent in the fetal position. To begin with, there's something unhealthy about people who are never sick. Every time they miss an opportunity to moan "I think I'm going to die," just loud enough for some loved one to overhear, they squander a chance to humiliate themselves. After all, how can we hope to tolerate our occasionally pathetic loved ones if we are not occasionally pathetic in return?

When your bed is your castle, maintaining pretensions becomes difficult. Pajamas are a great leveler. So is the fetal position. Because pretensions are what we employ to distance ourselves from others, we all need a bit of leveling every now and then.

My trouble began when the parcel service lost my computer and all my disks, precipitating a late-twentieth-century existential crisis. In sympathy with the disks, my back went out. Then I got the flu. Over the next week, my bed proved better than a Nautilus machine for the exercise of humility. It also turned out to be a laboratory for the study of self-pity.

For my first gambit, I attempted to parlay self-pity into compassion. "May I do anything to be of help?" my wife asked.

"No, [cough], I'm just fine, dear, don't worry about me [gasp]." She returned to her work.

Lying in wait for her return, I had plenty of time to plot a more aggressive strategy. Hours later, when she innocently passed through the bedroom, I sprang a stronger trap for her affections: the blatant moan. This did manage to catch her attention. She even sat down on the edge of the bed. But then she started offering useful advice.

As it turns out, when one is feeling rotten, helpful hints aren't always helpful. I didn't want advice. I wanted pity. Innocent suggestions, from "Why don't you take a shower? You'll feel better" to "Look through the Yellow Pages and call one of those places that rents lap-top computers," compounded my pain. Any intimation that I actually might do something to lift myself out of the doldrums seemed cruel, as if the whole, grim business were my own fault.

When down, one can always find ways to subvert potential sources of comfort. To parry my wife's sincere offers of practical advice, I grew irrational. Conjuring responses from the most perverse recesses of my mind, I managed to drive her away once again by telling her that because she couldn't possibly understand how terrible I felt, she should leave me alone. "It will be the best for both of us," I said. It certainly was for her. As for me, I lay awake for hours brooding over yet another abandonment.

What I learned during my week of convalescence is something that I keep forgetting. Self-pity defeats its own object. It is almost impossible to feel sorry for a person who is feeling sorry for himself. There is a simple explanation for this. When we are full of ourselves—whether with pity, fear, anger, ambition, or anything else—little room remains for anyone else to enter our lives. No one wishes to be the means to another's end. But when we make a play for pity, we insist upon just that. This leads directly to resentment, which compounds our self-pity and raises walls of estrangement between us and our loved ones.

When I awakened to this, I got up, took a shower, and phoned the computer place. It was humbling to admit that my wife was right, but by the end of the day my spirits had lifted, and she could abide my company once again. She even joined me in my castle, and in a true act of compassion let me beat her at gin rummy.

I felt like a king.

16

The Great Burden of Keeping a Secret

 Do you have a secret? I hope so. Life would be dull if we didn't have a secret or two. But watch out. Sharing secrets can be dangerous. Not only may our confidences be broken, but the moment we share a secret, we take our friends prisoner. Asking them to keep a secret not only puts pressure on our friendships, it also entangles them in conspiracy. Every secret kept is a potential cover-up. Remember, secrets are designed to keep others from learning the truth.

A few years ago I found myself in an awkward position. At our church we have a day school. The church was entering into negotiations with the school for an increase in rent, and I, as minister, was privy to preliminary discussions on both sides. The issue came up at a meeting of the church board. I told them I had just met with the school board and could share what I knew, but only on the condition that what I was about to say must never leave the room. At this, the chairman of the church board—one of my closest friends—flew into a rage. "Stop before you say another word," he said. "You know we wouldn't betray your confidence knowingly, but the burden you are about to place on us is one we shouldn't have to bear. Every word you say here, say to the world. It's the only way to ensure that none of us, especially you, will ever have to lie."

Talk about embarrassment. It was the moral equivalent of being ambushed. I was knee-capped by a friend. Humbled, I said what I was planning to say anyway, and then went directly to the school board and repeated it word for word. Everything turned out fine. More important, my conscience remained free.

The German philosopher Immanuel Kant coined something called the categorical imperative. The idea is simple: Whenever we speak or act, we should behave as if the whole world is speaking or acting with us. Whatever we do, imagine that everyone else is doing the same.

I used to make fun of this. Just think: What would happen if we all flushed our toilets at once? So much for the water supply. Not to mention what quitting our jobs would do to the world's economy. But that's not what Kant had in mind. His idea makes the golden rule concrete: when we do unto others, we should act as if they were doing the same unto us. So much for secrets. According to Kant's categorical imperative, the moment we share a secret, everyone would know. That's really what my friend was telling me. Though the door was closed, I should speak as if the whole world were listening.

This insight changed my life. I don't live up to it all the time, but whenever I start worrying that people may find out what I've said or done, I tell them myself before they find out from somebody else. One friend, describing this as "giving it to them before they can take it from you," says I'm not playing fair. And, in a way, she's right. Because few people play by these rules, it does tend to put one at an unfair advantage. Even as every lie gives someone potential ammunition against us, the truth, especially when self-inflicted, tends to be completely disarming.

The truth can be embarrassing, of course. For instance, due to my penchant for indiscretion, here are a few of the things that I have revealed to my congregation over the last ten years. I am a hopeless manager. I can't stand any meeting that lasts more than an hour. I prefer making snap decisions, even if they turn out to be wrong, to the lengthy process that improving them might entail. And I could live forever in a dirty building.

I still have a secret or two, of course. But my friends don't have to worry. My secrets are nothing special. Besides, I fully intend to keep them to myself.

17

A Lion's Lament

I attended a formal dinner this past week. You know the scene: Men dress up like waiters, women like tropical fish. This same discrepancy—drab males and colorful females—spills over into everyday life. Yes, some women don pinstriped suits for business, and the occasional professional athlete, secure in his masculinity, bejewels himself for battle, but as a rule, whereas men aspire to conformity, women seek distinctiveness in dress.

This first caught my interest when I was a little boy. One didn't have to be a budding naturalist to notice that, when it came to plumage, we humans were almost unique within the animal kingdom. For instance, to the untrained eye, most female birds of approximately the same size, regardless of species, have a dun, undistinguished look, whereas their partners sport outlandish, almost unnaturally vivid plumage.

The same goes for fish. When I was a boy, we had guppies. In fact, guppies figured prominently in one of my two, absolutely incomprehensible, man-to-man discussions with my father about sex. I have no idea what he intended for me to learn, but as I understood it then, males are colorful so that females will notice them; females are fat because they have babies in their tummies; and you've got to put the babies in a different bowl as soon as they are born, because their mommies are ravenously hungry as soon as they give birth.

53

As a young male, I took pride in the males of other species. My favorite role model was the king of the jungle. With his flowing mane, he cut a magnificent figure, his wife pallid by comparison, merely an oversized cat. When I discovered that she was stuck with all the work, my respect for him only grew.

I asked my father about this. As all fathers do, when he didn't know the answer to something he made one up. He told me that lionesses did all the hunting because the male lion, with his flamboyant coif, was too conspicuous. "As a matter of fact, I am a Leo, son."

"What's a Leo, Dad?"

He happily explained that a Leo is a particularly bold and decisive person with enormous leadership potential.

"What am I?" I asked.

"Libra, I think—a blind woman holding a scale—or maybe the goat."

It seems that Leos have trouble remembering other people's signs. It didn't matter. Even if I weren't a Leo, I could act like one. That night, as my mother was preparing dinner, I issued an ultimatum: "No more haircuts."

"You look like a girl," my father said three months later. I remembered that. In the years to follow, my hair remained long, but as soon as I could I grew a beard. This was in the late sixties, at the advent of the age of Aquarius, when young women dressed in faded, formless bedspreads, and my buddies and I, sporting dashikis, looked like male animals are supposed to look, flamboyant and wild. Now I'm older, equipped with a closetful of dark, all but interchangeable, pinstriped suits, and a haircut that should last me until spring.

I'm not sure it's an improvement. Nor is it fair. After all, I do most of the cooking in our household these days, and share equally in the child care. Yet my wife gets away with keeping her hair blond and wearing flashy clothing.

I did put on a garish, lime-colored suit jacket the other day. I found it in the back of my closet. It was my father's. Maybe real Leos can get away with this sort of thing. My wife made me take it off. It's now in a box, slated for the next charity pickup. Presumably, someone who can't afford to dress properly needs it more than I do. The blahness continues.

Watching the presidential candidates on television recently, I noticed that all twelve of them were in uniform: navy suits and red ties. I felt a twinge of nostalgia for the good old days when men were boys, and boys were males.

18

Live Free or Die?

 My nine-year-old son is making his first major solo flight, trekking twenty-five blocks into the heart of the city for a doctor's appointment. As a newly liberated father, I am terrified.

I think back to last week, when the two of us had fifteen minutes to blow in midtown Manhattan before Twig was due at his drama class. He asked me for a snack. Being bigger than he is, I confidently told him that instead we'd be investing our unexpected gift of time in a bookstore.

"I'll have a snack, you buy a book," he said. "I'll go to class on my own. I'll be okay."

"Come off it, Twig. I can't set you free at rush hour in the middle of the city."

"Sure you can, Dad." Then he hit me with a line that sounded very much like the truth: "Life without freedom is death."

The New Hampshire public relations office should press this kid into service. You know the slogan on their license plate: "Live Free or Die." I've always scoffed at it, but when paraphrased by my son, it made an infuriating amount of sense.

Won over, I entered the bookstore; he, the Three Guys Restaurant across the street. Twig got the better of the bargain —a slice of lemon meringue pie and a doughnut, with a glass of water on the side and a nickel's change. I squandered my own allotment of freedom squinting through the bookstore window, waiting casually to pounce the moment he emerged.

Upon arriving home, we held a family council. In a close vote, freedom triumphed over death. His mother and I administered a double helping of earnest advice concerning crazy cab drivers, anonymous child molesters, and seductive drug pushers, then granted Twig limited visitation rights to the city.

He just called to tell me that he had arrived at the doctor's office safely. One down, a million to go.

However great the bother of protecting our children, permitting them to protect themselves is far more daunting. The reason is simple. They have no experience in survival. We, on the other hand, recognize full well the dangers they face, knowing how lucky we ourselves are to have survived our own hapless youth.

Things get worse, of course. Eventually, I'll even have to permit my children to drive. The first summer I had a driver's license, I abused this privilege in every way imaginable. If life were fair, I would be dead. Every weekend, my friends and I descended upon Stanley, Idaho, population 35 (swelled on Saturday night by 500 real cowboys, their prospective dates, and one carful of dudes). The local sheriff looked and limped like Matt Dillon. He insisted that we stack our beer cans next to the dance hall instead of throwing them into the street. After dancing the night away, four drunk dudes would drive home along the Salmon River. Twice that summer I fell asleep at the wheel, only to awaken drifting off the road on the far more forgiving mountainside. Had my friends and I grown up in New Hampshire, with a little less luck our license plate might well have read, "Live free *and* die."

The same goes for all of us, grownups included. From little things like smoking, jogging in traffic, loading up on cholesterol, or driving without seat belts, to major league gambles like mountain climbing without a rope, recreational drugs, and casual sex, almost any imprudent act is dangerous. Every time we exercise our freedom, we risk abusing it. To complicate things further, folks who are eager to restrict freedom are potentially as dangerous as those who abuse it. Enforcing their own scruples, they defend freedom by insisting that others must act as they do, which often means succumbing to their fears.

The doorbell just rang. All aglow with accomplishment, my son has survived his adventure in the city. I can finish this in peace. But not really. His linking of freedom and death is more complicated than at first it seemed. Life without freedom may indeed be death, but life *with* freedom can lead to death as well.

Twig interrupted my reverie to ask, "Next year, can I walk around the city all by myself whenever I want?"

I just said no.

19

Expensive Thrills

When I was a kid, my friends and I took Monopoly seriously. Once we played for one hundred hours straight. We were going for the *Guinness Book of World Records*. There were regular updates on the local rock station, and we even got our picture in the newspaper. We held the record for five days.

I remember one particular game. I had a hotel on Park Place. My opponent landed there. He was smoking a cigar, our chosen form of adolescent rebellion. I was already counting my money, but when I looked down at the board, I saw that an ash lay in the blue rectangle where my hotel had been. "Sorry," he said. "No rent this time. Your hotel burned down."

Not that it mattered, but this young trader was a traitor. The two words are related. Both go back to a Latin word meaning "to hand over." Rolling the dice to turn over big money is a high-stakes gamble. Traders risk a loss, but traitors hand over something far more valuable. Put in the context of the Wall Street scandal, insider traders are traitors. They hand over their integrity and ruin the game.

Why does a man who earns a million or two a year break the law for a few hundred thousand more? The answer I've been getting is greed. I've tried to make that work, but somehow it doesn't compute.

Two years ago I had drinks with one of these characters, a

neighbor of mine. He turned out to be an insider trader, but back then he was just a Wall Street whiz. Looking back I remember that he certainly had no time for me or anyone else at the party. He was bored stiff, sipping a soft drink and watching the time, pleasing his pregnant wife as best he could, doing his familial duty. This, at the same time that he was meeting middlemen in alleyways and exchanging insider information for suitcases of cash.

Why do they do it? Is it greed? I don't think so. I think he was having an affair. Not with another woman but with money. Affairs are exciting. It's not the sex so much as the adventure. Meet me under the clock in the lobby at the Sheraton at 4:45. We'll find a quiet corner in an out-of-the-way restaurant and then go to a motel and register under someone else's name. Affairs offer romance in both senses of the word. They provide danger, intrigue, finally even regret and pain, each a reminder that one is still passionate and impetuous enough to risk everything on a single throw of the dice.

Think of it this way: You are married to your money. You have a great deal of it but still are not satisfied. Then one day someone comes along who offers you a little excitement—illicit cash on the side. It's a way to spruce up your life. Hot money. The amount doesn't matter. It's the risk, the danger, the rush of excitement when you call from a pay phone and hear from someone that you've just met that he'll arrange a drop at a men's room in Grand Central Terminal or sit behind you in the fourth car on the 6:30 train to Stamford.

The principal incitement here is not money, it is crime. After all—returning to my analogy—you can have sex with your wife or husband every night of the week, even register under your own name, have dinner in the window, hail an old friend across the room. What's so exciting about this? That's precisely the problem, of course. In a good marriage both partners discover that their relationship grows richer with each passing year, deeper, stronger, and more abiding. Yet many successful young people today, having everything, are bored.

Poor folks and those struggling through the middle class may have a difficult time conceiving how a six-figure yuppie would be bored, but some of them are. Yes, they have everything money can buy, which means everything but happiness. It's nothing worth feeling sorry for them about, only helpful to remember when trying to understand how a successful Wall Street trader may lapse into crime.

So far as I know, no women have yet been convicted of insider trading. But because women have affairs, I'm sure the time will come. One day she will become bored with her old familiar money and go out looking for a little excitement. It will be good for a while. Affairs always are. But she will answer for hers, too, just as my neighbor did. All I know is this: As with our spouses, when it comes to our money, it pays to be faithful.

20

Betrayed by Loyalty

 Benjamin Church was a loyalist. If he had been as loyal to his wife as he was to his king, he might have changed the course of history.

Somewhat perversely, it was my wife who brought Benjamin to my attention. Having stumbled across a volume devoted to the leading traitors of the American Revolution, she thought I'd be interested in getting to know one of my ancestors. Benjamin Church is the antihero of Chapter 2, ranked second only to Benedict Arnold. I was insulted. Benjamin should have been given the first chapter. After all, he was a traitor long before Benedict Arnold.

Benjamin was a doctor, poet, philosopher, and newspaper editor. With Samuel Adams's circle as his closest friends in Boston, Benjamin was privy to the revolutionary councils from the very beginning. As tensions grew between the colonies and the crown, he boldly decided to hurl himself into the breach between his monarch and his friends.

Benjamin's first gambit was as self-effacing as it proved to be ineffective. In his weekly paper, under his own name, he wrote half-articulate and unreasoned rabble-rousing articles calling for revolution. Then, under the pseudonym Tom Thumb, he wrote thoughtful, tightly reasoned replies arguing for restraint. All this did was to make him a hero among his friends. They promoted him to surgeon general of the Revolutionary Army.

At this point, he took more drastic measures. He wrote a series of letters in code to the king, begging him to lift the hated tax. To deliver these letters safely he had to entrust them to someone in whom he had complete confidence. He chose his mistress. This was a mistake. If you get nothing else out of reading this, remember that mistresses often turn out to be more trouble than they're worth.

She was caught, of course. They took her to Samuel Adams's house, where Adams interrogated her and decoded the letters. Benjamin was promptly arrested, tried, and convicted by revolutionary tribunal. The problem was, our nation was so new that we had no precedent to instruct us on how to punish traitors. Not wanting blood on their hands, our patriotic forebears removed Benjamin Church under cover of darkness and put him on the first boat to Bermuda.

Loyalty is a tricky issue. Benjamin was loyal to his king even as he betrayed friends. It's not likely, but had his messages gotten through, the cause of both might have been served. Let's say the king had relented and canceled the hated tax. Instead of being relegated to the second chapter in a minor book on traitors, Benjamin might have gone down in history as a patriot and hero who risked his life for a higher cause.

We have to be careful here. G. Gordon Liddy was loyal. Of all the figures in the Watergate tragedy, he was the most loyal. He gave his word and kept it. For this he spent more time in jail than any other Watergate defendant. Keep this in the back of your mind when you think about loyalty. There is loyalty among thieves, even as there is loyalty among patriots. But who is a thief, and who is a patriot? Depending upon your perspective, the heroes and the scoundrels are interchangeable.

The problem with loyalty is that its flip side, betrayal, always shadows it. Like duty (remember the Nuremberg trials), it is a dependent virtue. Not only are we judged by the nature of our loyalties but also by their consequences. It's not that we shouldn't be loyal. But when we're tempted in this noble direction, we should go a step further and ask ourselves this: Whom are we betraying? Another useful test is whether we stand to benefit from our loyalty. Will it advance us a peg in society or help us keep our job? If so, watch out. As a cover for self-promotion or protection, loyalty is more likely to be a sin than a virtue.

I'm happy to report that Benjamin Church was loyal in the old-fashioned way. He paid for it. His ship sank on the way to Bermuda.

III

CASES OF MISTAKEN IDENTITY

21

Our Many Names and Numbers

 People say that success in the late twentieth century demands at least a measure of computer literacy. A good sense of humor is far more important.

Don't get me wrong. I am a fan of computer lists, the fully automated post office, and dozens of telephone companies. After all, I am a clergyman. My duty is to love the unlovable. Besides, think of how far we have come since every piece of junk mail was addressed "Occupant." Back then, we were all nobodies. Today, we are a fascinating mix of characters, with dozens of different names and identities.

Take R. Roffester Church, for instance. Judging from the quantity of mail he gets, Roffester must be corporate America's main squeeze. Apparently, he is an avid outdoorsman whose special interests run from tents to plaid shirts, and who, if he could afford it, would subscribe to every rod and gun magazine, and vacation in Alaska. I get a kick out of this. After all, my idea of nature is the postage stamp of a park I look down upon from my sixth-floor window. Roffester provides me with a perfect alter ego. When I get his mail, I feel like a real man.

Another of my invisible housemates, whose existence is abbreviated as Crunch F., gets offered millions of dollars. "Yes, Crunch F., that's absolutely right, a 10 million dollar check in Crunch F.'s name could very well be yours just for the asking."

With my luck, and a name like that, if he ever does win, Crunch will keep it all himself.

And then there is the Church of Forrester. Ralph Waldo Emerson once said that "every institution is the lengthened shadow of a man." Well, friends, I've finally made it. As an institution, my needs are staggering. They run from state-of-the-art copying machines to T-shirts with my own logo on them for all my employees. Imagine how smug I feel, when my real church, the Church of All Souls, gets mail addressed to the Church of Poor Souls or the Church of All Sorts. Remember, this is an institution that has computer capacity of its own, which means that every tenth thank you letter begins, "Dear 10021." As one long-time member wrote, "Surely by now we know one another well enough. You can address me by my name and not my zip code."

The Church of Forrester is only one of my institutional pseudonyms. I am also the Forrest Church. Because my peculiar name (often misspelled) pops up occasionally in the *New York Times*, I was once immortalized in its Sunday crossword puzzle. The clue was "Chapel in the Woods," the solution, "Forestchurch." They spelled it wrong, of course, but as an experienced junk mail fan, I knew who they were talking about.

You may have noticed that the junk mail principle has now spilled over into telecommunications. These days one gets telephone calls even from computers. It's a little like being approached by the answering machine of someone you don't know. More often, someone's bought a list that includes one of our proxies. "This is John, of Acme Investment Services. Is Mr. Forrester in?" Perversely, I enjoy such calls. No one who knows either me or my net worth would ever waste his time pitching investment opportunities in my direction.

And then there are those wonderful old-fashioned wrong

numbers. When one of my ministerial colleagues, whose wife is a minister also, moved to our city, their family inherited a telephone number that recently had belonged to an "escort service." About eleven o'clock every evening, the parsonage phone would start ringing off the hook. One muffled voice after another would ask, "Is Jessica there?" The two teenage daughters of the household, more amused by this than their clerical parents, took to answering the phone, "Dial-a-Prayer."

I'm proud to say my home has never been confused with a bordello, but one recent wrong number did catch me up short. It was Saturday evening. I was working on my sermon. The phone rang. I picked it up. The caller said, "Hello, is Jesus there?"

22

Feeling Guilty When You're Not

Perhaps you don't have this problem. If not, you won't understand my dilemma. Whenever I look in my rearview mirror and see a police car, I feel guilty. I'm simply in the way, of course, driving the speed limit and holding up traffic. Yet for some perverse reason, I wait for the siren, struggling against the pathetic temptation to cut the suspense, pull over at once, and turn myself in.

It happens every time I receive correspondence from the IRS. Before daring to open it, I say my prayers. Imagine how I'd feel if I *were* cheating on my taxes.

My first major experience of authorized intimidation took place on my honeymoon. My wife, still cherishing the illusion of my manhood, sat with me peacefully in the waiting room of the Saint Thomas airport on our way home to Washington. Two officers approached. "Sir, please come with us for a moment. We have a few questions to ask." After seizing my pipe and taking it to a laboratory for examination, they proceeded to strip-search me for drugs. Even with my clothes on I am easily intimidated by people in uniform. You can imagine how effectively I pleaded my case in the nude.

As I pulled up my trousers, they brought another fellow in to suffer the same indignity, a tweedy professorial type. Furious, he read them his rights and demanded a lawyer. They asked him a couple of innocuous questions and let him go. I cooled my heels until my ashes returned from the laboratory. But his noble behavior emboldened me somewhat. I plucked up my courage and asked one of these forbidding characters what they were doing. It was obvious, of course. Members of the new Nixon "War on Drugs" commando squad, they were searching for pot.

"How long have you been at it?" I inquired.

"Four months."

"How many people have you apprehended?"

"No one, so far."

Returning to the waiting room, instantly I knew why. The tweedy fellow and I were the only two people with facial hair, mine a somewhat pathetic mustache, his a rather splendid beard. Clearly this was the government's number one criteria for identifying druggies, and every druggie knew it. I looked around at my fellow passengers. The room was full of potential criminals. Too rich and too thin, clearly some of them were now, or recently had been, high on something. After all, they had nothing else to do.

I learned little from this experience, remaining sensitive to even the most innocuous nod of authority, but a full decade passed before I was actually apprehended again. We were heading home after visiting my parents over Christmas vacation. As I drove up the New Jersey turnpike with my wife and son, a siren pierced the air, red lights flashed, and a cop pulled us to the side of the road.

It was bound to happen someday.

"Open up your trunk," he said. I fumbled with the keys, and finally got the lock to turn. He picked for a minute at the ham and turkey carcasses in the heavy iron crocks that, courtesy of my mother, were weighting down our rear, and then, without apology, said, "I thought you were running cigarettes." Running cigarettes? I have a hard enough time stopping smoking them.

I wish I were more secure, less easily intimidated, but still, this makes me wonder. Why do some innocent people feel guilty when unfairly suspected of a crime while so many guilty people unabashedly protest their innocence? Are we innocent folks more easily intimidated by authorities because we respect them more? Or are we simply more frightened of misbehaving or appearing to misbehave?

Guilt gets a bad rap these days. One ends up feeling guilty about feeling guilty. But what about all those cads who feel guilty only about getting caught, not because they did something wrong in the first place? If you suffer from my disability, think about that for a minute. Sure, we inflict some small harm upon ourselves. Our self-image and self-confidence suffer every time we wimp-out in the face of authority. But we don't hurt anybody else, and in this day and age that's not a bad thing.

23

The Wisdom of Inflatable Owls

What would you do if you had a nest of pigeons roosting over your front step? You might begin by consulting Harvard University. Its business school has made a name for itself by successfully pioneering the case method for teaching. They present the situation, then ask, *How would you respond?* The useful thing about this exercise is that whatever your predicament, before long you discover that things are not as simple as they seem.

To begin with, your front door is encompassed by a twenty-foot-tall arch, so the pigeons are out of reach. That's not the only problem. Three "pigeon control" outfits have come in with competing bids to poison the pigeons. Their bids vary widely, and the chosen instruments range from poisoned corn to deadly pellets. The real problem is, you cannot choose between them because your front steps are those of a church. In good conscience, killing pigeons is out of bounds.

Yet you have to get rid of them. Your minister greets his congregation on these very steps every Sunday morning. He is a sitting duck. Believe me, an accurate pigeon-dropping from twenty feet feels very like an egg would if it were gently cracked over your head.

So you seek a less deadly alternative. One of the three exterminators comes forward with what appears to be an acceptable compromise, halfway between killing the pigeons and being

73

fouled by them. That's right, poison them a little. They don't die; they just tend to go away.

Jumping at this solution, I arrived at church one Sunday and discovered to my horror that the steps were besplattered with broken eggs—real eggs—and tiny, dead infant pigeons. Their more hardy parents were still in place, and prolific as ever. I felt like a criminal, though not a successful one.

Harvard case studies don't often have a moral, but mine do. These pigeons are not unlike our problems. They roost over our front door, befouling our steps, and most of the time we don't know what to do. Because our problems often concern people, poison is out of the question—unless, of course, we want to make the cover of the *National Enquirer.*

Criminal chic is the rage these days, but the payoff is not worth the price. So we try a different gambit. We poison them just a little—a spouse, for instance—and end up wounding innocent bystanders, such as our children. Every day a little death, broken eggs, unintended victims of our petty search-and-destroy missions.

The problem doesn't go away. Lace a problem with half a deadly dose of poison, and like an insect that has learned to tolerate DDT, it will return even stronger and more pernicious than before. So that's not the solution. But happily, there *is* one. In fact, I have stumbled upon it this very week: inflatable owls.

Last Thursday we festooned an inflatable owl with red and blue streamers. We suspended it from our church roof with a line of twenty-pound test fishing leader. The pigeons flew out of their roost like a mad dog's breakfast. Not only are inflatable owls less expensive than poison, but they actually do the job.

So the next time you have a seemingly intractable problem —with your spouse or another loved one—consider employing an inflatable owl, some ingenious but nontoxic attention-getter.

If always surprising, they come in many guises. Try a spray of flowers. Or a game of gin rummy. Or a night out on the town. Go to an unimportant movie. Or a marriage counselor. Something different. It may not work, but it's worth a try.

Humor helps as much as anything. And, believe me, once your problems begin to take flight, it's impossible to look at an inflatable owl without laughing. Yet owls are wise, even inflatable ones. They help us solve our problems without resort to poison.

24

Let Us Now Praise the Pigeons of the World

I am in trouble. I have provoked the ire of an animal-rights advocate. This is no small matter. Professional animal lovers are a fervid species. In demanding repentance, they make street-corner evangelists look like pikers. My crime was against pigeons. What I wrote had nothing to do with pigeons, of course. It was about people, like you and me and the animal-rights advocate. Even so, most of us are insecure, and I am no exception. One sharp word of criticism can banish from my memory paragraphs of praise.

Not that criticism can't be turned to good account. Though the line between us has blurred lately, here politicians could learn something from the clergy. We in the clergy welcome opportunities to confess our sins. In this spirit, I offer my confession.

Friend of Pigeons, I repent. Forgive me for plotting to poison the poor innocent birds that were roosting over and befouling the front steps of my church. Not only do I repent, but here and now I shall restore the reputation of this much-maligned, if difficult to poison, creature, so long as you remember that this isn't about pigeons either.

I begin with a question. What animal springs to mind when I mention the following: (1) peace, (2) the Holy Spirit, (3) an obscenely delicious chocolate-covered ice-cream bar? If you answered "pigeon," you are correct, for that's precisely what a dove is, a member of the Columbidae family of birds, popularly known as pigeons. Gentle, plump, and small-billed, recognizable by the bobbing of their heads when they strut about, doves, according to the *Encyclopaedia Britannica,* "cannot be distinguished from pigeons either by size or by scientific classification."

I chanced upon this startling bit of trivia during an unsuccessful attempt to learn German by reading Luther's translation of the Bible. All I remember is that the word *Taube* (German for *pigeon*) kept popping up in odd places. For instance, when Noah elected one animal to fly from the ark and seek out dry land, he chose a pigeon. She returned with an olive branch in her beak. And when the Holy Spirit selected an earthly vessel by which to manifest itself hovering over Jesus' head as he was being baptized in the river Jordan, again it was a pigeon. Apparently, when God needs something important done, a pigeon gets the call.

I find this heartening. To begin with, most of us are pigeons who would like to be doves. Now we can look at the doves strutting by, bobbing their heads, plumping their feathers, and say to ourselves, "No big deal, they're just pigeons, no different from the rest of us." Beyond this, we pigeons hold a significant advantage. We are less likely to be impressed by the cut of our own jib. A dove may be tempted to flaunt some unsubstantial quirk of nature, like nationality or skin color, but we pigeons know better. Underneath we're all the same.

I have proposed the plastic owl as a gambit for solving domestic strife in a peaceable manner. But when it comes to world peace, let's not forget the pigeon. Real pigeons don't live unusual lives. They are monogamous, remaining faithful to their mate until he or she dies, and then slow to couple again. They share incubation, the female by night, the male by day. We tend not to pay them much notice. Unafraid of strangers until someone stamps his feet or claps her hands, the pigeon is also a survivor. Though not sufficient, survival is certainly necessary, and is threatened daily by people who spend far too much time building cages and stamping their feet, and not nearly enough remembering that they are far less different from others than they think.

There are 290 species of Columbidae—doves, turtledoves, all of them pigeons. I once fashioned myself a dove, but I like being a pigeon. Perhaps, if we get it right, "When the time of singing of birds comes, the voice of the pigeon will be heard in our land."

25

Advice from the Most Ignorant
of Men

 When she first came in to talk, she had not seen or
heard from her ex-husband for almost ten years. Out
of the blue he had called, said he was in town for two
days, and wondered whether she'd like to get together.

Their marriage had been a disaster. After a brief, phospho-
rescent romance, they had eloped, getting married in a tacky
love chapel in Las Vegas. Two years later she filed for divorce.

"Should I go out with him?" she asked. "I really hate him."

"Then you have to say yes," I responded, without any real
confidence in the wisdom of my advice. "It will help you get on
with the rest of your life."

At first she resisted. After all, he had robbed her of her youth
and broken her confidence. Even more than the impetuous act
of marrying, her failure at marriage embarrassed her. Those
among her family and friends who were kind enough not to
remind her that they had known it wouldn't work out surely felt
that way. As a result, she is still shy of commitment and unsure
of her judgment, especially about men.

She paused; I searched for something wise to say. "I don't

really hate him," she said softly. "I hate myself for marrying him."

I'm not a therapist. For one thing, the more I learn about life, the less I seem to know. Ignorance grows in direct proportion to knowledge. As Socrates once said, "I am the most ignorant man in Athens." Knowing as little as I do, I'm still far less ignorant than Socrates.

"Go see him," I said. "Then come back and tell me how it went."

She chose the time and place: three in the afternoon at a tearoom in an elegant hotel. The next morning she showed up in my office unannounced.

"What happened?" I asked.

"He is still as handsome as ever and was very nervous. He spilled his coffee on his pants. He was even more frightened than I was. I asked him about his life. He's doing okay, working in San Francisco, almost got married again but lost his nerve. I had a splendid time."

"You did?"

"Absolutely. We had two wonderful hours together. I remember now precisely why I fell in love with him. He's a winsome man, vulnerable, appealing. As I sat there listening to him talk, it all came back, our courtship and crazy dreams, my deep desire to protect him, to care for him, to spare him from the world. In fact, for the first time in ten years I am able to forgive myself for the terrible mistake of marrying him. If I hadn't done it once, I'm sure I'd do it now."

"Are you going to start seeing him?" I asked.

She laughed. "Absolutely not. It's suddenly so obvious to me. I've been kicking myself for ten years, but I couldn't have helped falling in love with this character, even marrying him.

But only once." She laughed again. I wasn't used to hearing her laugh.

"So you still love him, but you aren't going to see him again, is that right?"

"Of course I don't still love him. In fact, after two hours I knew perfectly well why I left him. It's one of the best things I've ever done in my entire life. This guy's a disaster. He's self-absorbed, needy, unable to concentrate on any problems other than his own. You know, he only asked me once about myself, and then changed the subject."

"That must have been hard for you."

"Not a bit. It reminded me that I have a life of my own now, a real life, not someone else's. It took me years, but I have a real, honest-to-God life."

"So leaving him was the best thing you've ever done?" I said. Wrong again.

"No," she said smartly. "Seeing him again was the best thing I've ever done. Thank you so much for helping me to understand what I had to do. Now I can get on with the rest of my life."

I didn't know what I was doing, of course. But, if Socrates was ignorant, who am I to boast?

26

Confidence and Compliments

Earlier this year, a friend of mine landed a new job as business manager of a small corporation. A month later her world was a shambles. She simply had to quit, she told me; that or be fired. For hours on the phone, we calculated the relative advantages of collecting unemployment or preserving pride. The next morning her company's president rendered all this moot. Calling her into his office for "a friendly little chat," he proceeded to offer some office-spun advice that is well worth sharing.

Let me tell you how she got into trouble. It stemmed from insecurity. She desperately wanted to establish respect among her co-workers and staff. So she didn't just start her job, she attacked it. She was relentless in pointing out what was wrong with the office. Among other things, she determined that at least one major position and several members of the support staff could be abolished without apparent consequence, save for the bottom line.

Did this endear her to her co-workers? Of course not. By the end of the month, not one staff member was eager to cooperate with her. Though polite at first, they quietly undercut her until, finally emboldened, they began to express their resistence more openly. Her desk became a bunker. Every time she came out from behind it, she got strafed. So when her boss finally called her in, she knew she was finished.

"Nothing much to report," he said. "I just thought you might be interested in knowing a little about my hang-loose managerial style. It's based on a simple premise. Every word of criticism weighs as much as four words of praise. All of us are insecure. It's hard to hear the criticism of another, unless we are assured of his or her respect. For example, when I assumed my first managerial position, instead of concentrating on what was good around here, I focused on what was wrong. I uncovered plenty of problems that way. But since I didn't really know anything about past efforts that had been made to solve the problems or the complexities that underlay them, my attempts were frustrated, and my work frustrating.

"Take Mary. I know you've had trouble with Mary. So have I. But, following an uncharacteristic display of patient observation, I found that people like Mary are more important to this company because of what they have contributed over the years than for what they are able to do for us today. Not that she doesn't serve in other important ways. By keeping her in her position, and quietly distributing her work to others, we show everyone who works here that we value our people for who they are, not just what they do. This builds spirit and inspires loyalty. Besides, as you too will surely discover, there's not a person on this staff whom Mary hasn't helped in times of personal need.

"It reminds me of my first memo, actually a manifesto, which addressed our needs brilliantly, if I do say so myself. There was only one problem. Unbeknownst to me, if implemented it would have devastated staff morale. I set out to identify and expose people's weaknesses, before troubling to discover and reinforce their strengths.

"Business, you see, is like a family. Within a family, members may freely criticize one another. But should an outsider dare to exercise the same privilege before being accepted as family, even when what he says is true, the family members will band together against him. I was still an outsider then. "You are one of the most able people I have ever worked with. Over time, I know, you will make your mark here, a fine one. I'm proud to have you with us."

Three months have passed. Things are far from perfect at the office, but daily they seem to be getting better. My friend has changed her style a bit, and slowed her pace. Yesterday she lunched with Mary, who is a font of information and fast becoming a friend.

Ironically, her boss was especially delighted with a memo she wrote on ways to improve office efficiency. Her co-workers helped her draft it. They were even able to accept an occasional word of gentle but well-deserved criticism. But what would you expect? After all, she is family now.

27

Shying from One Theory to the Next

I have a new theory: Almost everyone is shy.

When visiting a new church on Sunday, the man who cut a major deal on Friday hesitates before going downstairs to have coffee with people he doesn't yet know. The woman who recently spoke up in a public meeting, daring to criticize the school board, would do anything to avoid the pressure of attending an office Christmas party, where she would have to compete with others compensating for their own insecurity. The child who won a major school honor steps up to the podium—self-conscious, blushing, scared to death. Put us in an awkward position, and almost all of us turn out to be shy.

It's not a crime. How can we help but be shy? After all, we know better than anyone how inadequate we are. Ninety percent of us know that we are ill adroit, undeserving, and, in some obvious and painful way, unattractive. Deep down inside we know this, even when we are willing to admit that our self-criticism may in fact be no more insightful than the extravagant praise that absolute strangers, also shy and self-deprecating, seem hell-bent to lavish upon us.

I hesitate bringing this subject up. No writer likes appearing redundant. Having listened to "The Prairie Home Companion" for years, I am in awe of Garrison Keillor, who elevated shyness to a midwestern sacrament. He also turned shyness into a racket, however innocent, like selling milk to the parents of children.

But shyness isn't always pretty. Some joker jumps up at a party and starts dancing on the table. However lost in his cups, I swear that nine times out of ten he is compensating for shyness. If we remember this, we won't be too hard on him. He will be hard enough on himself the morning after. Just remember, he too is shy, shy enough to blush at his reflection in the mirror, even when no one else can see it.

Shyness can be debilitating; almost always it is embarrassing. But in its own way, shyness also is honorable. If pride ranks first among the seven deadly sins, shyness must be a virtue. To the extent that it is, shyness reminds us that our virtues often cause us far more pain than do our sins.

I speak from experience. Having veiled my shyness brilliantly for years, even today it often gets the better of me, especially when I'm thrown into a crowd of people I don't know.

Whenever I enter a room filled with strangers, I instinctively look for a corner or a bulletin board. Then someone notices me. All of a sudden my hands begin to grow. Should I hold them in front of me or behind my back, put them in my pockets, or let them dangle by my side? It's amazing how awkward hands become when we decide to let them hang next to our body.

My hands and I enter into an absurd dialogue. "Hands," I say, "whether we like it or not, we are now in play. Someone has noticed us. Should we approach her? Should we look for another corner or bulletin board? Or should we ask the shy person next to us where the restroom is?"

It's not that my hands and I don't truly belong or have no right feeling comfortable in this room. After all, I am the guest preacher for the morning in a small church where no one will see me again.

I duck into the restroom. One hour later I enter the pulpit. It's a little like dancing on the table.

You needn't buy my theory about everyone being shy, of course. In fact, you probably shouldn't. Experience has taught me that most of my theories are flawed. My wife is particularly effective in reminding me of this. When I told her of my latest theory, she replied, "Anyone as outrageous as you, who blames his misbehavior on shyness, suffers less from shyness than from massive self-delusion."

One of these days I'll come up with a foolproof theory. How about, all theories are false?

I can hear it now.

"Not all theories, dear."

Shy by nature, I resist the temptation to respond.

28

The (Im)perfect Primer

 If you are anything like the rest of us, you probably have developed a surefire talent for undermining your confidence by contrasting your weaknesses with other people's strengths.

For instance, a co-worker of yours is enormously creative. Overlook the fact that she has just broken up with her seventh husband, feeds a coke habit, and is on the edge of a nervous breakdown. Simply measure your creative capacity against hers and feel deficient.

Or let's say you have a friend who won the lottery. No, you haven't seen him smile of late. And he does seem a bit paranoid at times. But just think what you could do or be if only *you* had won the lottery.

You may not be prone to this little game, but most of us are. That is because, in a perverse sort of way, most of us are perfectionists. By this I mean, we select the finest traits and talents of everyone we know, fashion a composite (say, "creative, rich, beautiful, funny, famous, and kind"), measure ourselves against it, and come up wanting. All of which leads me to Rule Number 1 in Dr. Church's Primer on Perfection: *Covet thy neighbor's strengths, but overlook his or her deficiencies.*

Test it out. Let's say you are getting along pretty well in most areas of your life. You are a pretty good parent, a pretty good friend, a pretty good lover. You do pretty well, in fact quite well, at work. Well, forget about all that. Think about your failures, especially your silly little ones. How you gain weight when you diet. How every summer you take *War and Peace* on vacation and read Robert Ludlum instead. How you haven't been back to the gym since that day you let them talk you into a full-year membership with everything included.

The trick is to forget about all the things you enjoy doing and tend to do well. Think instead of something that you have no aptitude for whatsoever. Fix upon that as your ultimate goal in life. You will never reach perfection if you simply keep building on your strengths. Stop deluding yourself. Remember, fame, love, and true happiness are just around the corner. But to get there you must honor Rule Number 2 in Dr. Church's Primer on Perfection: *Overlook thine achievements. Instead, focus upon one or two prominent wants or weaknesses. At the expense of everything else, become obsessed by them.*

And that's not all. Let's say you drink too much. Or tend to procrastinate. Or hold grudges far too long for your own good. You could do something about these things, but how much easier it is to give up. Attribute your powerlessness to fate or, better yet, to the damage inflicted upon you by your parents.

On the other hand, there are things in our lives that we cannot change. Here's where the tried and true, if ever-frustrated, perfectionist really stands out. That is to say, if you are plain, aspire to beauty. If well educated, long for the simple pleasures of rusticity. And if you have trouble balancing your checkbook, dream about running your own business. If you work hard at it, my guess is that you will manage to jump into both of these pitfalls at once. Hence, Rule Number 3 in Dr. Church's Primer on Perfection: *Stoutly remain fatalistic with respect to all flaws, deficiencies, and foibles that might actually be corrected if only thou wouldst put thy mind to it; at the same time, set impossible goals for thyself and try to meet them.*

Talk about choices? You can place yourself on the rack of perfectionism by following but a single one of these three rules. As for myself—just a tip—I find it most effective to alternate them. But who am I to boast? After all, try as I might, I'm not perfect either.

P.S. Why is it that, having failed in our every attempt to achieve perfection, so many of us remain unable to forgive others for their imperfections? Just a question.

29

To Forgive Is Divine—and Human

Recently I received a long letter from a high-school acquaintance. I hadn't seen him, heard from him, or even thought of him in almost twenty years. His letter was remarkable and very sad. It told the story of his life. This story, recounting an intense struggle to overcome self-pity and self-hatred, hinged, in his memory, upon a single event.

He had been in love, and never happier. The young woman he loved thought she loved him. But she wanted to be sure, so she asked a friend about him. This friend cautioned her to be wary, for her boyfriend was known for his fickle ways. So she broke up with him.

Something like this has happened to all of us. A trust betrayed. A friendship compromised. The sad thing is that some people pick up their marbles, go home, and are tempted never to play again.

My old acquaintance is settled now—a successful lawyer with a wife and young children—but this single rejection, and his friend's betrayal, cast a shadow over his life that has never lifted. After all these years, he was writing to me because I was that friend.

I searched my memory. For the life of me, I couldn't remember this conversation. I couldn't even remember the young woman, by face or by name. He admitted that he had not confronted me at the time. Our friendship went on as it had before. If I acted wrongly in giving this advice, I had no opportunity to beg his forgiveness. This momentous event and its aftermath didn't register at all. Now, my old acquaintance was writing to say that after all these years—in and out of therapy, struggling with the impact of this one memory—he had finally discovered what he must do. He must forgive me.

I have to admit, at first I was irked. He was forgiving me for something I was not sure that I had even done. But as I reflected further, I realized it didn't really matter. Finally, he had gathered sufficient courage to confront me, and also the wisdom to forgive, to lay his anger and self-pity to rest. That is what mattered. How many of our lives are haunted by the specter of unresolved business? And how often could that business be taken care of by a single act of direct confrontation?

This may require subtlety. Most people don't take well to being told that they've destroyed your life. But however deep the wound, they probably haven't. This should make things easier, both for them and for you. Confrontation is painful, but it often leads to healing. A wound becomes fatal only if we refuse to have it dressed.

One of the twelve steps toward health followed by Alcoholics Anonymous is to go to people you have harmed, confess, and beg forgiveness. Even if your confession is not accepted, something wonderful happens. You know that you have done all you can to make amends. You finally can start down the path of self-acceptance. You are liberated, your energies freed to invest in love again.

It's a little like going back in time. Probably we would make many of the same mistakes if we had life to live all over again. But having visited our past (as we do with each act of forgiveness), we may return from it more able to accept our own and others' weaknesses, remembering that we are all imperfect sons and daughters of life and death, whose trespasses need to be forgiven, even as we need to forgive those who trespass against us.

And so I wrote to my old friend, and thanked him for forgiving me.

IV

A HALF-FULL CUP

30

Everyday Miracles

 Not all years are the same. Take 1988, for instance. Being a leap year, 1988 has one more day than 1987 did. This is no small matter. Days are important. On any single day our life can change dramatically: a chance meeting, an unexpected triumph or tragedy, a resolution to change that somehow we manage to keep.

Having an extra day this year also takes a little of the pressure off January 1. I wish I'd saved all the resolutions I've made on New Year's Day over the years. They'd constitute a small book by now, or a broken record, one I could take out whenever I needed further ammunition to prove to myself what a worm I am. I could call it *The Case of the Missing Backbone.*

The main problem with New Year's resolutions is that we tend to make too many at once. "This year, starting now, I'm going to quit smoking, get up every morning at five and exercise, stop eating dessert, call my mother every other day, have only one and a half drinks before dinner (for my heart), and write a novel." The engine that powers our character often needs more than a tune-up. Sometimes, it requires a complete overhaul. Even this can be accomplished over time, but we're not going to find a new driver.

For making resolutions, almost any day in the year is preferable to New Year's. Most days, we would be delighted to discover the resolve to accomplish even a single character-improving act. But on New Year's our tendency is to wipe the slate clean, committing ourselves to an impossible set of demands, only to wake up in the same old bed of crumbs.

To avoid humiliation for a change, this year on New Year's Day I resolved to spend a little quality time with my son. Twelve whole hours, to be precise. There were five bowl games on television, and we went gavel to gavel. I haven't abandoned hope for working needed changes in my life; I've just postponed it to a more propitious time.

Fortunately, we get an extra day this year. So the real question becomes, what are we going to do with it? Odds are, we'll end up wasting it as well. But that's okay. Remember, it's a free day, a bonus. If we waste it we don't lose anything. Besides, even wasted days are precious. Yet, if we keep on the ready, eyes open, mind alert, we may chance upon some perfect way to seize it. And what a splendid thing that would be. Like returning home after a long search only to find the treasure we were seeking planted in our very own backyard.

Why not start planning for our extra day right now? This doesn't mean looking for a new, more fertile field, but rather tilling the one we've got; sowing a few seeds here or there, not forcing flowers to bloom before their time; even weeding a bit, but not when the ground is frozen; and remembering to rotate our crops as the year goes by, to ensure that the ground will remain rich.

It's like preparing for a miracle.

Miracles happen, you know. Every day. But that's just it— this year isn't really all that different from any other. After all, what is one more day, when compared with the improbable miracle of any day at all? Still, an extra day is nothing to sniff at. In the only lottery that counts, it's one more opportunity to draw the winning number. This happens every time we awaken to discover how miraculous a day can be.

They don't often seem that way, of course. We tend to take our days for granted. Besides, we can always find some reason to indict them. Others disappoint us. We break our resolutions. We make a mess of things. Perhaps if we began each day by accepting ourselves and forgiving others, needed changes will come more easily.

We might even remember something we keep trying to forget. One day, not unlike this one, our gift of days will be taken from us. But that's okay too. All our days are free days, every one a bonus. Every one a miracle.

31

Talking to Cabbies Isn't
Always Taxing

 When my wife and I moved to New York, we gave up our car. We could have kept it—for the price of a one-bedroom apartment in Boise, Idaho—but we traded it for a taxi instead.

I've discovered that most cabbies are great. For one thing, they know where they're going, which is a welcome relief. But beyond this, they've got a knack for the ten-minute ride. They will tell you exactly what they think about almost anything, from U.S. foreign policy to the mayor's private life, from a game-booting error to the tragedy of the day.

Now that baseball is back, I've shifted my priorities, but during the winter doldrums, I asked cabbies about themselves. "How's business?" I said. As with all such polls, it was unscientific, but for a reflection of human nature, their answers were revealing. If you pose this same question, the response is likely to fall into one of four basic categories: 1—Get lost, 2—It stinks, 3—Same as usual, and 4—Great.

The first type of cabbie, a blessed rarity, blinks at you with disbelief, slams the plexiglass partition, and turns up his radio. For me, all this means is that I spend the entire trip self-consciously cowering in the backseat while trying to work up my courage not to tip. Thus far I've failed.

The second fellow jumps at the opportunity I've provided. He bemoans his fate. As it turns out, life is a conspiracy among the mayor, the taxi commission, the potholes, the passengers, the weather, and God, with him as chief victim, served up by cruel fate for daily slaughter. The problem is, it's hard to work up sympathy for someone who's dead sure that he's both wronged and right.

The third cabbie, representing by far the largest group, acknowledges that everything's basically okay. Today may not be all that great, but experience has taught him that tomorrow will balance things out. Sure, the traffic is lousy, but when it comes right down to it, driving a cab is just a way to make a living, nothing more.

Happily, there's a fourth type, as rare a bird as the first. He's worth waiting for. He opens the partition, turns off his radio, and waxes lyrical. "Business? It's great. It's always great. Don't let nobody tell you different." He's got pictures of his kids taped to the dashboard, and maybe a Saint Christopher medal too, or a pair of bronzed shoes hanging on the rear-view mirror. But most of all, he's got spirit. In fact, you've sometimes got to pray that he'll keep at least one hand on the wheel.

Cabbies may be special, but this is not an isolated pattern. Think about your co-workers, neighbors, or family. Some are so angry, they haven't got the time of day for you. It's as if they were saying, "Go ahead, just try to make me feel better." Don't. It's not an invitation. Others are looking for sympathy and quick to blame. Whatever's wrong, it's not their fault. Be careful here. Before you know it, it will be your fault. Still others have a stoic view—life is grim but manageable. Perhaps they've been around the block a few too many times. With such people, the best thing you can do is try to make them laugh.

Blessedly, however, a goodly number of our friends and

acquaintances fall into the fourth group. Somehow they manage to exult in life. Not that it's a bowl of cherries, simply a menu filled with possibilities. When the traffic is good, it is "great." When it's not, "not to worry." And when they ask you how you are, they really want to know.

So I find myself in this grimy cab with an unshaven, tough-looking character. "How's business?" I ask.

"Well," he says with a grin, "I woke up this morning, didn't I, so today's a good day, right? I got work. I can feed my family. We've got our health, thank God. So that's enough, right? How's your business, buddy?"

All of a sudden, we are talking about me. And so I tell him a bit about myself. We pull up to my destination. "It's been a privilege," he says. The privilege has been mine.

We'll probably never meet again, but the least I can do is contribute to the adage that happiness spawns happiness, and demonstrate that goodness is something more than its own reward. Paying a $3.50 fare with a $5 bill, I tell him to keep the change. And then I think about that line of his. Not a bad way to end a ride, or a day, or for that matter, a life.

"It's been a privilege."

32

A Story Too Good to Be True

Sometimes I hear a story that makes me feel sorry for novelists. You'd think a novelist could write her own ticket when inventing the truth, but the best stories are "too good to be true." No self-respecting novelist would touch them. The critics would kill her. Fortunately, I am not a novelist, so I can tell you the true story of someone who discovered that the old adage "No good deed goes unpunished" ain't necessarily so.

In the mid-1950s, the noted economist Eliot Janeway struck up a friendship with an international trader who sold lead and zinc and bought copper and coal for Yugoslavia. He was a shrewd businessman, but also turned out to be a colorful, engaging fellow. On the pittance doled out to Yugoslavian bureaucrats, he lived a Spartan existence in New York City with his wife and five-year-old daughter. His pride was such that he wouldn't let anyone, not even Eliot Janeway, pick up the tab at lunch.

One day Janeway said, "Why don't you jump the fence, go private, set up business here? You'd take the market by storm, and also get something back for yourself and your family, a little financial security."

"No, I have my honor, and am to my country thankful," he replied.

Shortly thereafter, Tito appointed a new chief of police, who undertook a review of all Yugoslavians living abroad. When this man's case came up, someone determined that he was living too high on the hog in capitalist America. Deeming this a security risk, they called him back to Yugoslavia and threw him in jail.

Before returning to Yugoslavia, his wife—a scholar—made a desperation call to Eliot Janeway, who, unbeknownst to her, makes his career by plunging passionately into issues of public concern whether invited or not. He told her to sit tight, picked up the phone, and called the head of the Department of Slavic Languages at Columbia University. Not only should they expand their program to include courses on Yugoslavian language and literature, but he had the perfect candidate. Fine, they said, as long as you pay her salary for the first year. And so he did.

Then he called Dean Acheson in Washington. The State Department was reluctant to intervene on such a minor matter, but finally Janeway prevailed, and the man was freed to return to the United States. He set up his own business, and, as Eliot 'predicted, was tremendously successful.

But that's not the story.

Two years ago, as happens to some people with diabetes, Eliot Janeway fell prey to a painful eye disease. He began to lose his ability to read, couldn't take glare, and suffered dry tearing. Remember, this is a man who reads two books and writes two articles a week. His eyes are like the hands of a precision machinist. Yet, the finest specialists in the world told him that in his case the condition was irreversible. He would simply have to live with it.

Then he remembered his old Yugoslavian friend, who shortly before his death had told Eliot how proud he was of his daughter. She had just completed Columbia University's medical school and had landed a job as a research opthamologist. On a lark, Janeway picked up the phone again. She reviewed his case and made a series of recommendations and referrals, and in a matter of months his eyesight had returned to almost normal. That is the story.

It won't work, of course. Too many coincidences. Too happy an ending. No one will buy it. But just try telling this to Eliot Janeway, who discovered firsthand how a long-forgotten good deed can come back to bless us.

Eliot still wears a rakish pair of tinted amber glasses to cut the glare. But, the miracle is, he can see almost as clearly as he did a quarter of a century ago, when he saw clearly enough to put himself out for a friend.

33

The Inspiring Effect of Praising Others

Have you ever received a compliment you didn't deserve? I've made a career of it. Among other things, it has spared me from being a perfectionist. For me, it started early. My parents were indiscriminate. It's not a bad thing. With every compliment, they were saying that they loved me. Once I knew that they loved me, it wasn't so bad being spanked.

Most of us have sense enough to doubt ourselves. But if everyone else doubts us, we are lost. The great thing about compliments is that they give us another chance. They inspire us to try things again, even dare to do them better.

Criticism can be helpful, but often it isn't. I notice this especially in meetings. Someone risks a new thought, and people jockey to be first in pointing out "We've tried that before" or "It simply won't fly." So much for new ideas. We learn this trick in school. Criticism is a cheap way to establish superiority. Somebody else does the work. Our job is to rip it apart.

Some criticism is justified, of course. And not every compliment is complimentary. For future reference, I offer this brief bestiary.

Begin with the senatorial compliment. Like a skunk it waves its tail before it spews. "I want to begin by thanking my distinguished colleague, the senior senator from the great state of North Carolina. . . ."

And then there is the Social Register compliment, catty condescension aimed in a chilly tone at the hat or coat or dress of some "inferior."

In marriages, there is the backhanded compliment. ("Dinner was *unusually* good tonight, dear.") This is the praying mantis of compliments. After making love it bites off the head of its mate.

Not to forget the compassionate compliment. This is the ostrich of compliments. We reserve it for people who are dying. We don't know what to say, so we tell them how wonderful they look.

But what about the real thing? Apparently we think that whenever we honestly praise another, we diminish ourselves. Is someone keeping tabs? If I compliment you, do I lose a point and you score one? Are we superior to people whom we criticize, and inferior to those whom we praise? In fact, the opposite may be true. When we pour out compliments, our cups run over. But when we try to save every drop of our precious nectar of praise, it evaporates, and soon our cups are dry. Ironically, a readiness to criticize may reflect insecurity. People who are sure of themselves are generally much more capable of complimenting others than those who need to prove that they are better, smarter, more reasonable, or wise.

If you are confident enough to wish to break the pattern, you might try this: The next time your husband or sister or boss or assistant has a "brilliant" new idea, find something kind to say before you put it down. In part it's a game. No criticism without a word of praise. Find something good about a bad idea and it will change the way you listen. It may even change the way you think. Think about what happens when somebody compliments you: You have two clear choices. Only one of them is correct.

If somebody compliments you, do her a favor. Accept. When she compliments your cooking, don't tell her that the dinner really wasn't all that good. When she thanks you for sending a thoughtful note or visiting her in the hospital, don't tell her it was nothing. It wasn't nothing. It was splendid.

I learned this from my parents. When it comes right down to it, it makes no difference whether we deserve a compliment or not, because each time we are sincerely praised, the person who praises us shares in the pleasure. So enjoy it. And let them enjoy it. Which is simply to say, there is only one proper response to a compliment.

It is "Thank you."

34

Insecurity Issues

Sometimes our major security issues in life are really insecurity issues. I think of one friend in particular. He's very successful. Not only that, he's hard-working, high-principled, and, in many ways, unselfish. If you have a problem, he'll go out of his way to help you. But for some strange reason, when he himself has a problem, he finds a way to make it worse. For one thing, he has trouble with criticism. He doesn't rise above it or even learn from it. In fact, he takes every word of criticism as a personal assault. On the surface, it's hard to figure. Things are going well in his life. But deep down he's insecure.

One particular woman in his office has been giving him trouble lately. She is outspoken and opinionated and rarely agrees with his ideas. She doesn't threaten his job. She's in a different department and lower on the corporate ladder. He rarely sees her more than a couple of times a week. The problem is he can't get her out of his mind. So he has declared war. His memos are like heat-seeking missiles. He works on them until three in the morning.

My friend is so obsessed with this woman that he has finally provoked his co-workers' concern. They support him on most things, but they're starting to worry about his behavior—and his memos. "This is overkill," they say. "Forget her. You'll get most of what you want. Lighten up." As far as he's concerned, the difference between him and them is that he cares more about the company than they do. As they see it, he is losing his perspective. It's as if, to protect against shoplifting, he would be willing to bankrupt the store.

But he won't give in, and his stubbornness has cost him allies. People are beginning to come to her defense, some of them in his own department. In his search for honest ground, he has discovered quicksand. The more he struggles, the deeper he sinks.

In some ways his life reminds me of American foreign policy. Do you remember when Vietnam was our number one security risk? For ten years we fought to hold a beachhead there against Communist aggression. We spent fifty thousand lives and billions of dollars. It doesn't really matter why we failed. Perhaps we didn't have the will to win, as some people say. Or maybe we never really had a chance. What matters is that shortly after we stopped fighting for Vietnam, it disappeared from the map, not the world map but the map of our consciousness and concern. Instead of being thrown into dire peril for having failed in our mission, once we left Vietnam it ceased to be a security risk almost overnight. Judging from recent policy in Latin America, we have yet to learn the lesson of Vietnam. Neither has my friend. The more he struggles with his problems, the more stuck he gets.

The same is true of me. Most of my security issues are insecurity issues. When someone confronts me, I am tempted to answer according to my fears. A single ounce of confidence would probably work the cure, but instead I too thrash about in quicksand.

As for my friend, he is starting to cool off. But still he can't let go. This will be hard for him. He believes he is right. As he sees it, to back off now would be not only admitting defeat but also abandoning the truth.

Admittedly, I know only his side of the story. But, even playing devil's advocate, it seems that he may in fact be right. Even so, let's say he does prove his point. A full-scale confrontation with this woman, right now anyway, would clearly serve neither him nor his company. It would only divert everyone's energy from more important tasks. He asked me what I would do. I counseled nonintervention.

We can't play other people's cards, of course. Our own hand is tricky enough. But we can point out that when it comes to self-destruction, they, and only they, hold all the aces.

35

"Are You Okay?"

 I have a friend who always complains whenever I ask him how he is. "How are you?" I ask, my automatic pilot in perfect repair.

"Terrible. My back is a mess, and last week my neck went out. All of which is only slightly less disconcerting than the bill I just got from my urologist."

Not that he's exaggerating. A youthful sixty in aspiration and energy, he has cut out tennis, which he loves, and he missed his vacation last year, confined to bed with a back that wouldn't work. Even so, when I ask a person how she or he is, I don't really expect an honest answer. "How are you?" is like "Hello," the sort of greeting we offer to passing acquaintances when we are running late for an appointment. So you can imagine my surprise when I ran into this fellow on the street last week and asked him how he was.

"Fine," he said. I was in a hurry, but this caught me up short. Stopping in the middle of the sidewalk, I pulled him into a doorway and said, "What did you say?"

"I'm fine."

"What do you mean you're fine? Last week you had a brace on your neck, and today you're walking with a limp."

"Let me tell you something," he replied. "It took me years, but I finally got the message. Whatever may be wrong with me, most people up the ante, protesting that they are worse off than

I am. "If you don't believe me, when someone asks you how you are, just dare say 'My neck hurts' or 'My back aches.' Chances are you won't get commiseration; you'll get one-upmanship. You'll have to suffer through hearing about the other person's neck, back, anything that directs attention and sympathy to him. It's apparently reflexive, this tendency to compete rather than empathize. So I've made up my mind. Starting this week, when I'm asked how I am, I'm going to say 'Fine.'"

"What about your neck brace?" I asked.

"I no longer wear my neck brace in public because I'm tired of hearing tales of other necks, other joints. From this day on, as far as the world is concerned, I'm fine."

Having given up competing with others over pain, he reversed field entirely. Somehow he had managed to find a way to suffer other people's pain without compounding his own. After all, pain is a popular subject only when we are speaking about ourselves.

"All this got me thinking," he said. "You know my doctors never complain about how they feel. It's not their job. Their job is to make others feel better. And it's not a bad job, when you think about it. So you know what I'm going to do with the rest of my life? I'm going to empathize with people in pain. I feel that pain. I know how much it hurts. And I know for certain that they have as hard a time as I do getting that across."

"How are you going to do this?" I asked.

"Never again am I going to say 'How are you?' when I don't really want to know. And when I do want to know, I'm going to ask 'Are you okay?' For some reason, when you put it that way, people tend to be honest. And when they start to tell me how bad off they are, I'm not going to compete with them, just listen, even if they're better off than I am. And then I will tell them how terrible it sounds. And they will feel a little better."

"What about you?" I asked.

"I will feel a little better too."

I tried this out last week. It turns out that most people say they are fine when you ask "How are you?" But if you ask them "Are you okay?," if they're not, they unload.

Even as a minister I can take only a certain amount of this; so after five days I am choosing my shots. But it's still a funny thing. When I slip and say, "How are you?" and someone tells me the truth, part of me resents the intrusion. Yet when I ask "Are you okay?" and someone tells me that she's not, for some odd reason I want to know why.

36

When Opposites Attract

The old excuse for odd couples is that opposites attract. I don't put much stock in it. Judging from casual observation, the average husband and wife are roughly the same hue, proportionate in height, and compatibly shaped. More often than not, they share similar tastes, and unselfconsciously reinforce each other's prejudices.

Even those things that differentiate them seem conducive to their mutual pleasure. Talkers are compatible with listeners. And if one drinks when the other doesn't, there's always someone in the family to drive home. But in one respect this overworked saw does seem to cut straight down the grain. I may be projecting, but as far as I can tell, those of us who were born with a desperate need to be on time are drawn like flies to people who will do almost anything to ensure that we will be late.

Take a snapshot of my own marriage. On any given evening that we had plans to go out, it would picture my wife characteristically standing in the bathroom in her slip putting on her makeup. Wearing my raincoat and hat, I would be holding vigil in the bedroom.

"Are you ready, honey?"

"Do you have eyes, sweetheart?"

Only for my watch.

"Relax, I'll be ready in a few minutes." Time enough for a day's worth of exercise pacing in the hall.

Maybe it's because she's half Jewish and I'm half Presbyterian. One of the first marriage ceremonies I ever performed was between a Presbyterian groom and a Jewish bride. A half hour before the appointed time, the groom's entire family had stolidly aligned themselves in the front four pews to await the beginning of the service. Forty-five minutes later, the bride's family began to trickle in. Her grandmother was the last to arrive. As we scurried to jump start an engine that was almost dead, she seemed pleased by the attention, but didn't begin to understand what the fuss was all about.

Probably, my wife was born late, but she also may have been influenced by living, as a little girl, for three years in Peru. In Lima, the first party her parents were invited to was scheduled to begin at 8 P.M. They arrived at 8:30 and proceeded to cool their heels for the next hour, while their hostess steeped in her bath. Finally, the other guests began to arrive. By 10:30 the house was full. Dinner was served at 11:00. Latin time is the opposite of daylight savings time. Whatever the invitation says, add two hours, and then, for good measure, arrive late.

Punctual people with casual spouses may find parties painful, but airports are the worst. I am a prudent fellow. I like to arrive at airports at least an hour, maybe two, before my plane lifts off. Check in. Have a couple of drinks. Relax in eyesight of the gate. For some odd reason, my wife considers this a waste of time. Apparently, she gets a kick out of running from the counter to gate 94.

On the other hand, I have to admit that my penchant for hyperpunctuality inconveniences everyone, including myself. This is especially true on those rare occasions when, against monumental odds, I score a victory and manage to drag my wife to a party on time. The problem is, despite my inability to be late, I know as well as she does that it's impolite to arrive for a party on time. So, in full sight of the whole passing world, we sit together in the lobby on an ornate bench not designed for people, waiting forever for a handful of minutes to pass. I bite the bit; Amy holds the tether. Finally, I can't stand it any longer. It's ten past the hour. We arrive at the party, and pretend we're in Peru.

I'm never going to change—that much I know—and neither is my wife. But it has taken me eighteen years of a basically sound marriage to discover that, when opposites attract, to live together happily, opposites must forgive.

37

Saying No Can Be the Best
Yes in Life

Most of us begin practicing failure at an early age. We get our basic training in elementary school, little leagues, and serious discussions with our parents. For me it was the Boy Scouts. When I signed up, my uniform looked just like everybody else's. Two years later, no one would guess that we belonged to the same troop. My uniform hadn't changed, but my friends had won so many merit badges that theirs were like Joseph's proverbial coat of many colors.

Blessedly, I grew up with a high tolerance for failure. Though it continues to serve me well, back then it was essential. During two long years, I earned only one merit badge. Not a tent, fish, or deer, but a needle and thread. My sole accomplishment as a Scout was the blue-and-gold potholder I wove for my grandmother.

It doesn't hurt to fail at an early age. Things can't help but get better, and the company is good. Einstein could hardly speak. Edison couldn't add. Churchill wouldn't behave. And not a sewing badge among them.

Over the years, failure becomes more significant and potentially more devastating, especially for those who have a low failure threshold. One of my young friends won every merit badge in the book. It came easily for him. It was the story of his life, until he became an alcoholic. Only then did he score his first real success: He joined Alcoholics Anonymous.

For many of us, drinking is pleasurable. It releases tension, lubricates conversation, and lifts our spirits when we need a lift. But the same thing that makes alcohol appealing makes it dangerous. Beginning as our servant, it can make us its slave. When this happens, we must overcome both a habit and a physiological need. Becoming addicted to alcohol is easy. One may want to stop but be unable to. Yet people do stop. It happens all the time. From some deep reservoir of latent strength they say no and prevail.

Most alcoholics have known the very pith of human failure. Marriages have broken up, jobs been lost, health broken. But then, instead of playing for double or nothing, they refuse to throw in their last chip. Not with superhuman strength but with human strength drawn to its fullness, a ringing no is sounded, and with that no, a yes. A "Yes, I can." A "Yes, I must." A "Yes, I will." And with that yes, exacting the utmost of human willpower, a life is saved.

Four years ago, my friend was in the hospital in an alcoholic coma. After visiting him, I gave him up for dead. But he surprised me. He lost his wife and his job but not his life. Piece by piece, he put it back together. Such triumphs make most of our failures and subsequent successes look like child's play.

Having succeeded, recovering alcoholics thrive and serve, often without ostentation or any sense of superiority. Not only do they have a special compassion for the failures of others, but also they are living examples of our extraordinary power to remake our lives, to light a candle against the darkness and keep it burning.

I can think of no victory more stunning than the recovery from alcoholism or drug addiction. That's because few defeats are more devastating. But what about the rest of us? Since all of us fail, the recovering alcoholic may have something important to teach us. The secret is this. At times, the only thing to do with our pride is swallow it.

Not one of us is self-contained, wholly self-correcting and self-sustaining. Those who have tasted life's bitterness, only to be cleansed by the sweetness of a supportive family or community, are not ashamed of failure. It is nothing compared with the victory that is gained by turning to others and seeking their loving support.

Recovering alcoholics have learned to accept their weakness while looking beyond it for some greater power whose strength they might tap. Among the places this power certainly resides is in other people. I have known no recovering alcoholics who have not, at their point of greatest weakness, turned to others for help.

Which reminds me of the other lesson I learned as a Scout. When lost in the woods, if at all possible we should find a stream. All we have to do is follow it, and soon we will be home.

38

Turning Down Booze with a Smile

Dozens of the members of my church are also in Alcoholics Anonymous. They are conspicuously good church members, too: active, outgoing, understanding of other peoples' troubles, always ready to help a person in need. Like most ministers and rabbis, I am delighted when anyone joins my congregation, but these people are special. They seem to know how sweet life's fruit can be.

Most recovering alcoholics possess an additional gift, the ability to mingle unselfconsciously with others. Veterans of daily meetings where even strangers are encouraged to speak openly about deeply personal things, they reach out with ease to people standing in corners, to self-conscious folk who can't seem to finesse their piece into whatever puzzle they find themselves in. This is all the more impressive because at most parties the puzzle is cut in such a fashion that recovering alcoholics have to work far harder than the rest of us to find a comfortable fit.

Basing my evidence upon a whirlwind tour of holiday bashes, in almost every instance liquors and wines beckon from attractive bottles lined up on top of the bar, while the soft drinks—excluding demurely packaged, lightly perfumed mixers—are tucked away underneath. As for the coffee, "It will be ready in just a few minutes."

Smaller parties can be even more daunting. For some

strange reason, certain hosts seem insulted if one won't join them for a "drink." I secretly believe that this has less to do with "having a good time" than it does with the notion that sobriety is a downer for all concerned. Of course, should one happen to be the only sober person at a party, time does have a perverse tendency to stop somewhere between dip and dinner. It leads one to wonder, "Am I the only hungry person in this room?"

No great expert on discrimination against nondrinkers, I tend to drink defensively at holiday parties: that is to say, too much. My sympathy for nondrinkers is won during Lent and vicariously during the rest of the year through my wife. We drink gin and tonics: mine unadulterated by tonic, hers uncontaminated by gin. Still, I have managed to scrounge together a few pointers for anyone besieged by a red-nosed holiday host intent upon lubricating unwilling guests.

If you don't want to appear wimpy, I suggest the macho response: "I've already consumed a fifth of scotch today, and that's my self-imposed limit."

For health-conscious yuppies who still have a reputation to maintain, this may not work. As an alternative, try this: "Do you have any diet cola? I made a bet with my sports trainer. I'm going to lose a pound a day between now and Christmas. It's a long shot, but if I win, she'll give me a free massage before breakfast every day for a week."

This may offend your spouse or date, however. If so, you might employ a more socially responsible gambit: "I'm sure that you've noticed, as I have, the growing number of homeless and hungry people who live in the shadow of our opulence. During the holidays, for every drink I turn down, I intend to contribute five dollars to my local soup kitchen."

In certain company this won't work either. I can imagine a desperate host offering fifty bucks to the poor, if only you promise to match him drink for drink. What we really need is a foolproof response:

"I'm driving, and never drink when I drive."

"My doctor has told me not to drink."

"I have some important work to do later this evening."

"I find that drinking before dinner takes the edge off my appreciation of good food."

"It's kind of you to offer, but frankly, I don't enjoy alcohol."

Try humor first. But if your host turns out to be a sobersides, get serious and say "No, thank you."

39

Is Happiness in the Cards?

 Where does happiness lie? Is it in the cards we are dealt or the way we play our hand?

Anyone who tells you the cards don't matter—that in the game of hearts you can always sluff off the queen of spades or shoot the moon if you are sharp enough—is a fool or possibly a rogue. By suggesting that everything from illness to poverty can be corrected by "right attitude," today's pop gurus and sleight-of-hand healers toy recklessly with the lives of those whom they lure into their pricey weekend seminars.

Mesmerizing the credulous with pretty crystals, obscuring the reality of death in fantasy tours through imagined past lives, preaching peace of mind tricks as a cure-all, they trivialize suffering by blaming the victim. Yet, some people find that New Age elixirs, little liver pills for the soul, deliver at least part of what their hucksters promise. The philosopher William James called it the will to believe. Positive thoughts can be self-ratifying, even as our doubts, if deeply enough held, tend to be confirmed over time.

Had the little train said, "I think I can't, I think I can't," it never would have made it up the mountain.

I had two pastoral encounters this week with single women in their early forties. One was depressed, to the point of wishing she could chuck it all; the other lay in a hospital bed recovering from major surgery for a life-threatening tumor. In many ways, at birth these two women had been dealt much the same hand. By nature intelligent, attractive, and energetic, they were raised in large, upper-middle-class suburban families. Augmenting their natural attainments with discipline and hard work, each flourished academically and went on to succeed at a young age in business.

And both lived alone.

"I just can't stand it anymore," Emily told me. "My life is as barren as my womb. Without a family, my life has no meaning, and I've given up, absolutely given up, on ever having one."

On such occasions, I too feel helpless. Having long since abandoned dispensing platitudes to people in pain, I just listen and sympathize. Because she alluded to suicide, I wouldn't let her out of my office until she agreed to enter therapy, but that was about all I could do.

"I'm desperately lonely," she said as she left.

"Of course you are," I replied.

Then I went to visit Margaret. The lab tests hadn't yet come in, but the surgery seemed to have gone well. No surprises. Until she began to talk.

"I've had lots of time to think. Because of this operation, it's clear now, I'll never have a baby. No use pretending anymore, believing that somehow if I just hang in there everything will work out. But I'll tell you something, Forrest. You're always gushing on about relationships in your sermons. I know you don't mean only family relationships, but sometimes those of us who aren't married hear it that way. Once or twice, I've felt diminished by that, as if I were a misfit or cripple for not being married."

"Of course you're not."

"Yes, I know that, you idiot." She smiled broadly. "Especially now. I have a wonderful life, and I want to keep it. My work is great, and my friends even more special than I realized. Everything's more special. Even myself. This time in bed, just lying here in solitude, it's been amazing. I'm really in touch with things. I never thought much about death before. But now more than ever I don't want to die. I have so much to live for."

If loneliness is the emptiness of being alone, solitude is the fullness of being alone. Same hand, different plays.

I still don't know what to do for Emily. Given the way she is feeling, the happy talk of some seductive guru might do her good. But Margaret doesn't need rose-colored crystals or a soul map to ancient Egypt to find happiness. She's discovered it on her own, in the reflective solitude of a hospital room, her life triumphant, illumined in the shadow of death.

40

Choosing to Be Happy

Sometimes it seems that happiness rests at the top of an endless golden staircase. Somewhere near the top stood J. Paul Getty. At the end of his life he cursed his wealth and said that he would trade it all for one happy marriage.

The quest for happiness is fraught with such pitfalls. Public people lament their loss of privacy. Millions of unknowns dream of being famous. Beautiful people find reasons to regret their beauty, plain people their plainness. One man chafes under the restrictions of a marital covenant. Another mourns the emotional barrenness in a life of one-night stands. One woman, a homemaker, wishes that she were as successful as her neighbor, a businesswoman. Right next door, the object of her envy envies her the husband and children that she herself has sacrificed for a professional career. Just where you'd think the grass would surely be green, it is dying.

I am no longer startled by this. What startles me is precisely the opposite. So often, where you'd think that the grass would be dying, it is green.

A man is struggling with alcoholism. Everything in his life is going to have to be rebuilt from the ground up. He hasn't had a drink for two months. And he is happy.

A man's wife is dying. She has been given a week at most to

live. They lie together in their bed, talk about old times, look at family pictures. And they are happy.

Adversity doesn't always bring out the best in people, but it can. Perhaps this is because adversity tends to strip away our illusions. We are forced to work within tightly drawn and well-defined limits. When this happens, everything within those limits is heightened. Little things take on a much greater importance.

Last winter, sailing south on a beautiful ship, I awakened early one morning and went out on deck. The salt air was brisk, the sky a canopy of clouds. One other passenger was standing by the rail. "Lousy day," he said.

And then a deck hand carrying a bucket and mop, an old man with a bright red face and a Cockney accent, came down the stairway singing at the top of his lungs. A rousing, slightly off-color ballad it was, and my fellow passenger took great offense. What offended him was not the song so much as the singer. "Hasn't the bloke got eyes?" he muttered and then, confronting him directly, said, "What do you sing on a good day, a dirge?"

"A good day? Why, this is a good day."

"You've got to be kidding. I paid a lot of money for this, and what do I get? I might as well have stayed home."

"Guv'nor," the old man replied, a twinkle in his eye, "there's many a blind man who would give his eye teeth to look out on this day."

Call it thoughtful wishing. How often the happiness that could be ours today pales in comparison with the ideal that dances in our dreams. Perhaps, like this matey, we should think to wish instead for something a little bit closer at hand:

The courage to bear up under pain;
the grace to take our successes lightly;
the energy to address tasks that await our doing;
the meaning to be found in giving of ourselves to others;
the patience to surmount things that are dragging us down;
the comfort to be taken in opening our heart to another;
the joy to be gained even in the commonest endeavor;
the pleasure of one another's company;
the wonder that wells within the simple fact of being.

41

Crying in Our Cups

 In the National Museum in Jerusalem, I came upon a mysterious collection of tiny ceramic cups. It turns out that these were sacramental vessels. People cried into them.

Think about it. Your mother has just died. Or you have learned that someone you love has cancer. Or your wife has left you. Or you are struggling at work. More likely, you have simply broken down. Without warning, something hits you hard and you burst into tears. So you pick up your tear cup, put it under your eye, and weep into it. When you are done weeping, you cap it and put it away again. It is a way to save your tears.

Why save them? Because they are precious. It doesn't matter why you cried, your tears are still precious. They show that you care. A full cup of tears. You have felt deeply, suffered, and survived. In fact, if we knew better, we would cry far more often than we do. Life is difficult. We pretend that it is not, that we can breeze through. Yet not a week passes that we don't have something to cry about.

Men have a particularly hard time with this. We are taught not to cry. Tough it out. Don't let the bastards get you. Well, forget about the bastards. Think about yourself. If there is a single person who doesn't have something worth crying about, I would like to meet him.

I don't cry very often, but I know that I can. Sometimes I cry during particularly wrenching news stories, even commercials —put a kid in a commercial and I am a goner. So I know that I can cry. But when something happens that cuts closer to the bone, I close up. I protect myself. Even when my father died, it took me a full week before I finally could break down and cry.

The main reason we have such a hard time crying is that we are afraid of our feelings. Every time we express ourselves emotionally, we risk losing control. On the other hand, if we get too good at maintaining control, the results can be even more disastrous. We take our feelings and strangle them. And then we are nothing but closed flowers, tight and frightened little people, pretending that we have grown up and hoping that no one will notice how deeply we really do care. At first it is an act, a hard act, but over time, as we get better at it, it becomes less difficult because we really don't care any longer. If we don't practice caring, and hurting, and crying, over time we forget how.

There is something to be said for this, of course. That something is invulnerability. The word means "not susceptible to being wounded." The best way to protect ourselves from being wounded is to avoid love or to love only in little ways so that when we are hurt we will hurt only in little ways.

There is another advantage to bottling up one's feelings so that they will never spill over into tears. We get a reputation for being strong. As the song goes, "Big Girls Don't Cry." And we know about big boys—tough, macho, invulnerable. No tears.

By the way, there are two kinds of tears—tears of sorrow and tears of joy. For this reason the ancient Hebrews kept two tear cups on hand, one for when they were sad and one for when they were happy. Back then people were not afraid to cry. Their tears were sacraments of love, of caring deeply, of being alive. The fuller both cups were, the more a person was esteemed. Great-hearted people, it seems, cried far more readily than small-hearted people. Life touched them more deeply, not only the pain of it, but also the joy.

Anyway, there I was, in Israel in the museum. I wanted to cry. I wanted to pick up one of those little cups and cry my tears into it, to save them, to remember them. I thought how wonderful it must have been for some man who simply couldn't cope any longer—the pressures, the hurt—and so he went to his cupboard, picked up his cup of tears, and wept. He wept into his cup of tears until he could truly say, "My cup runneth over."

V

THE AVAILING STRUGGLE

42

Moments of Awakening

 When spring comes, the first thing I do is dust off my caps. Over the years, I have built up a modest collection: CBS Sports, Mack Truck, Jimmy's Feed Lot—that sort of thing. If you happen to be a minister, as I am, or, unimaginably, have risen to even greater heights, let me offer you a piece of advice. Go to your local five-and-dime and buy a silly cap. In springtime, people who attempt to maintain their dignity are a drag on everyone else's line.

Spring is a season for jesters and children. When she pokes up her pretty head and bursts into laughter, she's not only laughing with us but also at us, at our smugness and fears, our precious little rules and tight-lipped resignation. Goodness knows we need it. After all, how many springs do we get in any given lifetime? Surely not so many that we can afford to squander one. Spring is the most precious of seasons.

Summer, the season of ripeness, is certainly pleasant; life is regnant then, its beauty in full flower. Fall is the season of spreading waistlines and thinning hair, of harvest and dissolution. Winter is the season of wisdom and death. Each has its moments, but spring is different. It is the season of rebirth and awakening: life out of death; flowers from husks; Phoenix from the ashes. This can happen when we are fifteen, forty, or ninety. We're never too old for spring.

Let me tell you something about jesters and children. They

may not have a somber bone in their bodies, but they take the world seriously. Ships in the river, a late morning moon, crocuses, and daffodils: each is an event.

"Look, Daddy!" How often do I have to interrupt my important business at the utterance of these two wonderful words.

As for jesters, the fools of April, they too see things that the rest of us don't see. After all, they have little to lose by plunging merrily into the heart of things. But what *about* the rest of us? When we wake up in the morning—and what an astonishing thing this is—do we even blink at the wonder of it all, save to wipe the sleep from our eyes? No, we turn on the radio, get dressed, go to work, eat a couple of times, listen to the news, and drift off to sleep again. Think about it. When was the last time you went to bed and prayed, "If I die before I wake . . ."?

This is yet another reason for spring. In springtime we celebrate the great Western festivals of redemption, rebirth, and renewal. Freedom from bondage, life out of death, awakening from sleep to dream again.

Think of redemption as a coupon. In face value, it's worth nothing, a tenth of a cent, they say. But when you cash it in, you receive something of real value. Even as she laughs at us, spring shouts this from the treetops: "Cash yourself in. The world needs you. This incredible world of jesters and children, saints and scoundrels, desperately needs you to awaken to the miracle of being, and act upon the promise that is yours."

Forget it, you may say. What's there to cash in? Average looks, average intelligence, average job, average life? Well, don't forget it. Instead, look out upon your hard-edged, sophisticated city at winter's end—dead, drab, empty of life—and then, in three weeks' time, the whole place is a riot of bud and flower.

Yes, I'm being naive. I'm wearing my silly cap and looking

foolish and dreaming of a pennant, but so what? Spring is a season for fools and children. Right now, even Cub fans are intoxicated with hope. And why not. Springtime is a time of surprise, even when we know it's coming, a time of rebirth and awakening. The weather breaks, buds burst, and jesters and children remind us of what we keep forgetting.

Life is a gift and not a given.

Every day is a new day.

One day, not unlike this one, we will go to sleep and not wake up again.

But until that day comes, we could do far worse than to trust the jesters and children of spring, who awaken us to life's wonder and help us dream again.

43

Confessions of a Repentant Racist

A few nights ago I dreamt about getting mugged just outside the Prince George welfare hotel in New York City. Twelve hundred kids live in this dive, a real horror show, much worse than my dream was. Members of my church are active there, and I'd dropped by the day before to see what they were up to. It was impressive. But then I had this dream.

Leaving the hotel, I couldn't catch a cab, so I started walking, faster and faster, right down the middle of the street. Suddenly I found myself in an empty parking lot, alone. For some reason, I had my wallet in my hand. I offered a dollar to the first man who approached me. It wasn't enough. Instantly I was surrounded, desperate, frightened to death. What embarrasses me most about this dream is that I tried to protect myself by confiding to the people threatening me that I was a clergyman. They couldn't have been less impressed.

Then an odd thing happened. There were so many of them, and so much confusion, that I managed to slip away. In my flight I encountered a woman who also was looking for a cab, waving her arms, running down the middle of the street. The chances that both of us would escape were nil, so I asked her where she was going. "The Upper East Side." My destination too—Manhattan's gold coast, rich, familiar, and safe. We jumped into a taxi together. And then I woke up.

It won't surprise you that my dream muggers were black and this mystery woman white. It was your basic racist dream.

Two nights later, I attended a small, posh dinner party. Everyone was talking about Tom Wolfe's new novel, *The Bonfire of the Vanities*, a story about racial polarization, brilliantly written, without a hint of hope. They all loved it. One woman said, "Don't worry, we're going to be all right. The Hispanics hate the blacks and vice versa. They'll never get together."

Were it not for my racist dream, I might have let this pass. But I was frightened by my dream, and by this conversation. The currents of fear in our society run so deep. How in the world are we going to live together? So I proceeded to ruin the party.

Thank God for my daughter and P.S. 158, an old battleship of a school overrun with children of every flavor and color. The very next day, I attended a talent show there. My six-year-old daughter was featured. She and a friend had worked up a number called "The Doughnut Shop" (something I didn't completely understand about a doughnut and a nickel each having holes in them). They don't vote on winners at P.S. 158. Given the competition, this is probably a good thing.

Among my favorites were the Latino third-grader singing "La Bamba," with his little white buddy on the sax; a stirring rendition of "Blue Suede Shoes" sung as a trio by two first-graders and a kindergartener (two energetic boys—Italian and Irish—trying to keep up with a black girl twice their size); "Edelweiss" from *The Sound of Music*, performed by the daughter of the assistant U.S. attorney; the pop song "Donna," —"I've got a girl and Donna is her name"—hilariously sung by a little Greek girl; and the only pure-bred WASP in the bunch belting out "Somewhere Out There," a song about an immigrant mouse. But the real tearjerker was "Carry Me Back to

Old Virginny" played on the piano by a second-grader from Japan.

I admit it, I'm naive. So naive that this talent show gave me hope. Knowing that debunking is the rage these days, and debunkers feast on naifs, I wouldn't dish myself up on their platter had a friend of mine not told me about the first record in history that sold a million copies. It was "Carry Me Back to Old Virginny," sung by that good old girl, the opera diva Alma Gluck. Anticipating her little Oriental follower, she had come from Eastern Europe to find her fortune in this country just a few years before.

If my dream about getting mugged indicates that I'll probably go to my grave a repentant racist, the talent show at my daughter's school suggests another dream: harmony—with a dash of humor—between disparate races and faiths. I'm not so naive as to believe that this dream is going to come true. But I know one thing for certain. It's the true American dream.

44

Meditation upon the Death of a Child

I knew only this about the young couple driving me to the airport. Just before Thanksgiving, they lost their eight-week-old baby. No one knows why she stopped breathing, but she did, another victim of sudden infant death syndrome.

Their minister told me the story. When he arrived at the emergency room, the baby was barely alive, having been revived and placed on a respirator. The doctors held out no hope. As he and the child's father stood helplessly by, her mother sang to her baby. Sweetly and softly, she sang her favorite hymns: "For the Beauty of the Earth." "Transience." "Autumn Fields." My colleague, who has been in the ministry for nearly fifty years, had never seen anything like it. The following morning, she requested that these same hymns be sung at her daughter's funeral.

As we traveled together toward the airport, exchanging pleasantries, I tried to summon the courage to bring the subject up. This shouldn't have been difficult. I do it all the time. But, for some reason, I couldn't muster the necessary presumption to shift our conversation away from the weather and the morning's news. But then they asked me about my family. "Do you have children?"

"Yes, a boy and a girl."

"How old?" I couldn't go on.

Just as I was about to tell them how sorry I was about their baby's death, the young man said matter-of-factly, "You should know that we lost our infant daughter this fall."

"I do know," I replied. "Irving told me. Nothing is more tragic than the death of a child."

"It's interesting," his wife commented from the backseat. "Sometimes I get the feeling that other people have a harder time dealing with it than we do. It's so real to us. We know what we've lost. But other people can't face it. They can't talk about it. They're frightened."

"They're frightened of us too," her husband added, "as if we had some kind of disease that they might catch if they got too close." *Or said the wrong thing,* I thought sheepishly to myself.

"I know exactly what you mean," I said. "In this liberated age, the only taboo left, the only subject almost no one dares to talk about in polite company, is not politics or sex or religion, but death."

"We're doing pretty well," he continued. "Cathy's right about that, but we sure could use some help, and not just from the therapist we're going to. On any given day, one of us may need to work on the past, just as the other is trying to break free from it and focus on the present or make future plans. Yet with the whole world, our family and friends, tiptoeing around us, we are left almost wholly dependent upon each other. Sometimes the resources just aren't there."

"It's funny," Cathy added. "Though most people can't seem to handle talking about Sally's death, and are awkward around us, even shy sometimes, when we are together with them, laughing or chatting about some silly thing, I get this odd feeling that we're being judged, as if our behavior were somehow inappropriate."

"Perhaps we should wear black and not speak to anybody,"

her husband said and laughed. "That would take them off the hook."

We went on talking together. About the conspiracy of silence concerning death. About how the most natural thing in the world has been turned into a monster that people are frightened even to name. About Sally. About their decision to try to have another child.

Just before we reached the gate, I said, "You know, in God's eye, Sally's life is just as precious and blessed as your life or mine. Whether eight weeks in duration or eighty years, when viewed in the light of eternity the length of one life is indistinguishable from that of any other. What really matters is that she taught you something about how precious life is, and how much we need one another. Even in her dying, Sally touched and changed her little corner of the universe."

"You may be right," Sally's father said to me softly.

"I know one thing," her mother added in a bright, clear voice. "Now, when someone I know loses a loved one, I'll be there with a casserole and all the time in the world."

45

Bringing Yourself as a Gift

For me, walking into a hospital is like going outside on a winter's day. Before crossing the threshold, I brace for the chill of inadequacy that nips at my confidence the moment I pass through the doors. Over the years I've made hundreds of pastoral visits, yet hospitals never fail to intimidate me.

I head for the information desk, advance slowly through the line. The phone rings. I wait. Finally the attendant cups her hand over the mouthpiece. I mention my friend's name. She asks me to spell it. A Rolodex file spins. She shakes her head and asks me to spell it again.

Am I spelling it right? Am I in the right hospital? "Eight-one-four Woolman Pavilion, follow the blue lines." Returning to her call, she hands me my ticket of admission, a large pink visitor's pass with tattered edges. As a minister I don't really need one, but I take it anyway. I don't want to explain.

I walk down the hallways, following the blue line. I feel conspicuous, as if I didn't belong here. I'd like to put the visitor's pass in my pocket, but it's too big.

There are six elevators. By the time one arrives, a hallful of doctors and nurses are waiting with me. Squeezing in, I back myself against the wall. I am in the way. Fortunately someone pushes 8, so I don't have to ask. People nod at one another, but no one speaks. Instead, we watch the elevator lights tick off.

144

As I approach 814, I try to keep my eyes from wandering
into open doorways. It seems an invasion of privacy. Yet my
mind is filled with peripheral images, mechanical beds, ban-
daged flesh, hollow eyes. I reach the room, door cocked ajar,
silence within. Taking a deep breath, I hesitate before entering.

Surely I'm not the only one who finds hospitals forbidding.
In large part, this anxiety stems from fears concerning our own
mortality. Everywhere we look we are faced with reminders of
pain, sickness, and death, all the more haunting in the context
of a hospital's imposing impersonality. Yet someone we care
about is ill. We are bringing ourselves as gifts. When we arrive
at our friend's bedside, we must break through this veil of
impersonality and our own protective armor to ensure that our
discomfort doesn't prevent us from comforting.

Both patients and colleagues have helped me with this. Perhaps some of the things they have taught me may help you as
well. First, once you have greeted the person you are visiting,
sit down. If you remain standing it looks as if you're ready to
leave. Besides, since you don't stand when visiting a friend in
her living room, pay her a like courtesy here. Not only will this
make your visit more relaxed, but you will be at eye level with
your friend. All day long, people hover over her bed, looking
down on her. Give her a break. Have a seat.

Second, be sure to touch her. In hospitals, touch is often
invasive. It hurts. Touch is the probing of sensitive organs or the
insertion of an IV. For this reason, nothing soothes like the
loving touch of a friend. Smooth her brow, run your fingertips
down her arm, hold her hand.

Third, let your friend set the tone and subjects of your conversation. Try question/statements such as "It really must be
difficult?" This will permit her to lead the discussion wherever

she chooses. And don't be afraid of silence. Your presence speaks for itself.

Finally, if your friend is seriously ill or in considerable discomfort, don't stay too long. Ten minutes, sitting down, holding hands, talking quietly, is just about right. The quickest way to wear out your welcome is by lingering to prove how much you care.

After hundreds of visits, my discomfort in entering hospitals and negotiating their stark hallways remains. I have to face it —when it comes to hospitals, I'm basically a wimp.

Yet when I walk out of Room 814, the hospital doesn't intimidate me any longer. After a good visit, it never does. I know I belong. I even chat with nurses on the elevator and thank the attendant profusely when I return the pink card. Leaving I'm always glad I came.

46

Kindness Doesn't Kill

I just said good-bye to one of my parishioners, perhaps for the last time. A lovely man, he is dying in a stark V.A. hospital room in New York. We talked about his memorial service. "This may strike you as silly," he said, "but, just perhaps, could you sing the Navy hymn?" It didn't strike me as silly at all.

"And my ashes, I hope they will be cast onto the waters, spread over the waves of the sea. I have a friend who has a boat, but he may be out of town."

"We'll find a boat," I said.

"You know," he said and smiled, holding out his withered hand and pressing it into mine, "I love the sea. And I love the Navy. Isn't that silly?"

"No, certainly not, not silly at all."

"I never fought for my country, but I was ready to," he assured me. "Thank God, I didn't have to. Not for me, of course."

"Of course not."

"Not for me, for my country." We held hands as he drifted off. Once his breathing was quiet, I left his room. How tremendously sad. Another of my parishioners, young and beautiful, is dying of AIDS.

He is at peace, both with himself and with death. He told me so, and I believe him. But the rest of us are not at peace. The

AIDS epidemic threatens to tear this country apart. Sometimes a public issue becomes intensely personal. That is what is happening with AIDS. Among the fundamental choices that each of us faces is how we are going to respond to the AIDS crisis.

I can tell you how I feel. I am scared. For three years now, my congregation has sponsored an AIDS task force. Countless times I have been told, and have told others, that the virus can be caught only by a direct exchange of bodily fluids. Still, I am scared. This afternoon, visiting my dying parishioner, I felt unclean when leaving his room, as I always do when visiting a person with AIDS. I wanted to wash my hands.

If irrational, my response was real. The same is true of our government's reaction. With the exception of Surgeon General Koop, whose sense of balance on this question is absolutely masterly, most of our leaders feel the same irrational fear that I sometimes do.

Prudence is one thing. This week my dental hygienist wore plastic gloves. But then I saw a line of police wearing gloves. Where do we draw the line?

Our church put four thousand placards into subway cars and buses in New York. With charcoal drawings of a child, woman, and man, the placards read: AIDS: THE MORE YOU UNDERSTAND, THE MORE UNDERSTANDING YOU'LL BE; AIDS IS A HUMAN DISEASE. IT DEMANDS A HUMANE RESPONSE; and TREAT A PERSON WITH AIDS WITH KINDNESS. IT WON'T KILL YOU. Messages such as these might well be repeated across the country. Messages of compassion, of solidarity. For when it comes right down to it, the opposite of love is not hate. It is fear. As President Reagan rightly said, our battle is against the AIDS virus, not the people who have it.

If this epidemic spreads, as some experts suggest it may, punitive legislation singling out one or more of the minority groups in our society could soon impinge upon the rights of all of us. If we take even tentative steps toward a quarantine, before long this whole country will be quarantined. This was the experience of a friend of mine who's single who recently went on vacation in Europe, looking for a good time. When people discovered that she was an American, they blew her a kiss good-bye.

AIDS is deadly but not the most deadly of viruses. Yes, it can kill the body, and we must do everything we can to counter it. But there is another virus even more deadly. It kills the soul. Not only the individual soul but, if an epidemic of bigotry and fear should break out, the soul of our country as well.

There is hope, of course. We might begin by loving one another and our country as deeply as a certain dying sailor I know.

47

Strong Hearts and Strong Shoulders

When Cassie came into the world, three generations rejoiced. First, her parents. With a new, hard-won appreciation for the miracle of life, they had cause for great thanksgiving. Her grandparents too had special reason to celebrate. On one side she was the first grandchild, on the other, the first girl after four boys. As for her great-grandmother, she laughed and said, "Clearly, I haven't lived too long."

Cassie was three months old before her loved ones suspected that something was terribly wrong. She ate well, and cried her little heart out, and looked as beautiful as a baby can look, which is very beautiful indeed. But she didn't respond to bright colors or loud noises, and couldn't raise her head. After weeks of inconclusive testing, Cassie's parents had their worst fears confirmed. She had been born with a rare congenital disease. Special medications might help, but some of these, like steroids, could be given only in limited doses, to protect her kidneys from secondary complications. Beyond this, little hope was offered.

Cassie's father is a realist. "How long does she have?" he asked. Having seen such tragedies unfold before, I knew he might have posed this question differently. "How long do we have, and what are the odds on our making it?"

"Five, ten years. One never knows," the doctor replied. The watch began.

A wonderful little boy in my congregation died last summer. He too was born with a rare disease, which wouldn't go away, no matter how hard his parents prayed or his doctors tried. When I first met him, he was almost four and making progress. No, he couldn't talk, but he could walk a little, respond readily to others, and take real delight in life. Always the first to see McDonald's Golden Arches from miles away down the highway, he knew as well as any four-year-old how to wangle his parents into stopping. They, in turn, lived for the slightest breakthrough in his precious development.

But that's not all they lived for. They also lived for each other. Even when their son began to fail. Even when, after suffering a series of setbacks, he became completely disabled and finally homebound, they struggled and they thrived.

Thrived is probably too strong a word. But that's what the world saw. Two attractive people, outgoing, active in their local church, attentive to their friends, successful in their work. The world has strong shoulders, but there are lots of people who wouldn't think to cry upon them.

Even so, this couple surely has problems that the rest of us fail to perceive. Having seen it happen before, I sometimes worry that their son had become their primary bond. He was central to their existence, demanding so much from each of them that without him they may now have to struggle to rebuild a new life together. Of course, many things I worry about don't come to pass, even as things I should have worried about do.

Still, however well or poorly they fare, people with disabled children astound me. I find it hard enough being the father of two healthy children. And being the husband of their mother. We thrive too, of course. But the world seems to have no idea how difficult it is.

So what should I say to this young couple, hoping against hope, facing the diminished life and almost certain early death of their baby daughter? Perhaps, only this: Be gentle with each other, and forgive the world." Blessedly, we tend to rise in response to tragedy. Whatever hand we may be dealt, perhaps because it's our own hand, not someone else's, we play it far better than anyone else ever could.

But what if we don't? If we fold under the pressure, what then? Well, that's okay, too. If we can forgive the world for our pain and ourselves for our failure to endure it, a forgiving world will embrace us. We can lean on its strong shoulders, and cry our little hearts out.

48

Snatching a Victory in the Final Moments

 I watched a football game not too long ago between Saint Louis and Dallas. The Cardinals were two touchdowns behind. Their offense managed only a field goal against the Cowboys during the first fifty-eight minutes of play. Yet, launching into their final two-minute drill, Saint Louis scored three touchdowns and won the game.

However improbable, this reversal doesn't hold a candle to that of a man I knew. With far more than a game hanging in the balance, his own "two-minute drill" was nothing less than miraculous. With time running out, he recovered his old fumbles and scored a victory in death that had eluded him for a lifetime.

The old man was dying, and so he summoned his children to his bedside to tell them good-bye. Dutifully they assembled, apprehensive less because of his impending death than of his forbidding life. With family members related to one another by bonds of mutual estrangement, feelings had been strained for years, muted by pretense, insulated by formality.

In times past, whenever the old man had engaged members of his family in serious conversation, he had managed to direct the subject to his will. He seemed to think of his children and grandchildren principally as beneficiaries. They addressed him as "Sir." Always proper, he was like a silk glove on an iron fist, one of those people for whom it would have been much easier to write an obituary than a eulogy. His accomplishments were many, but all in the public domain: a brilliant business career, success in government service, renown as a philanthropist. Respected by all who knew him, feared by many, and loved by none, he served humanity through his industry and generosity, yet apparently had no inclination to establish intimacy with anyone. None of those who remember his late, stately wife recall ever having seen the two of them touch, even accidentally. But now he was dying, and one by one he called his children to him.

"John, I have not given you the respect nor shown you the love that you deserve. I know how much this hurt you, though you never seem to show it. In that respect, you are just like your dad. But in other ways, you've far outstripped me. Please know that I am prouder of you, and all the things you have done, than I am of my own accomplishments."

"Dorothy, when your mother died, a part of me died with her. The pain was so great that I retreated in self-protection from everyone I loved. Probably because you are so like her, I retreated from you most of all. I never had the strength to tell you. If only Mother and I had given you a glimpse of how deeply we loved each other, so many of your problems might have been avoided. I'm sorry. I love you."

"Billy, I know you have rejected all the things I seem to value—position, money, status in society. You won't believe this, but I almost did the same thing myself when I was your age. But I didn't have the courage. Please don't let anyone force you to be someone you are not. To me, you will always be the man I might have been."

Then the old man called the whole family together, addressing all the rest of them, each in turn. He took out a thick book of clippings and letters, filled with his grandchildren's accomplishments, their wedding pictures, academic awards, and stories recounting triumphs on the athletic field. Who could have imagined how deeply he cared? Leafing through it page by page, he told them each how proud he was.

As the evening went on, they began to exchange stories, laughing together, and crying a bit too, in relief as much as pain. He told them tales of his youth, especially of his deep passion for and devotion to their mother and grandmother. Then he kissed them each good-bye. They returned to their homes. He died a short time later. As one friend told me, "The old man finally accomplished in death something that eluded him in life. He brought his family together."

As the saying goes, "In life, as in football, the score at half-time doesn't matter." It may not be fair, and the odds may be long against it happening, but all it takes to turn a bad game around is a spectacular "two-minute drill."

49

Do You Want to See? Then Turn Out the Lights

You are sitting in the middle of a brightly lighted room, furnished with hopes and broken dreams, honors and failures, from yesterday and long ago. It is your life. Crooked pictures on the wall. Trophies. Unfulfilled expectations. Unexpected fulfillment. Little tokens of affection, perhaps in need of dusting. And the books of your life, remaining unopened or half read, tales of who you might have been packaged in the tattered covers of who you are.

Behind you on the counter is a stack of unwashed dishes—unwanted memories, deeds done in haste or left undone. And on the desk, lists, vows to change, old resolutions, hidden from full view but not completely forgotten, the folded corners and yellowed edges of your past. Finally, on the table, before your eyes but just out of focus, lies some tomorrow's paper, open to the obituary page.

Sitting in the middle of this bright room that is your life, you look out a window—your window on meaning—and try once again to figure out what it means to be alive and then to die. The problem is this: Outside it is very dark, so all you can see is your own reflection. Your window upon meaning is a mirror.

When things are going well, our rooms papered in dreams-come-true and hopes for tomorrow, we don't worry much about not being able to see out. But sometimes, after a personal tragedy perhaps, or—in some ways, more unsettling—for no particular reason at all, we look in the mirror and see only chaos. Even if we have everything in place, none of it seems to fit together. At times such as these, dark nights of the soul in the bright room of our lives, we are transfixed by the mirrored shambles, unable to divert our eyes, and tempted to pick up a stone and cast it at our reflection in the glass.

It's like the story of Narcissus. In the original fable, a young boy falls in love with his reflection in a pool, reaches out to embrace himself, falls in, and drowns. Surely people like that exist, but the narcissism I encounter, in my own life and the lives of my parishioners, is rarely driven by self-love. In fact, by definition, narcissism is not self-love but self-absorption, which often manifests itself as self-hate. We stare at our reflection in the pool, hate what we see, and are tempted not to embrace but to strangle it. It's like throwing stones at mirrors. When we get lost in our own reflection, so lost that we can imagine escaping only by destroying it, we might try turning out the lights.

This can be frightening. However grim things are, even when we hate what we see, our reflection has the advantage of familiarity. When we turn out the lights in the room of our lives, we can no longer see ourselves in the mirror. It becomes a window once again.

At first we sit in darkness, our eyes unused to the sight of nothing. But look closely. On the other side of the window, one by one the stars begin to come out. We still don't know exactly what they mean, but there they are, awesome and mysterious. Sometimes, it is all we can do to keep from reaching out to another person and saying, "Have you seen them? Have you seen the stars? I have, from my very window. Come with me and look."

And when we turn the lights back on, we discover that something amazing has happened. Yes, the dirty dishes remain on the counter, and the pictures still hang crooked on the wall, but it somehow doesn't matter quite as much as it did before. Call it the grace of God or whatever you will, but our temporal worries diminish in the context of eternity, reawakening us to the wonder of life and death, reinvesting our lives with meanings to be shared.

As Oscar Wilde put it, "We are all in the gutter, but some of us are looking at the stars." Or, as they say on those energy-saving reminders, the next time you are lost in self-absorption, "Please remember to turn out the lights."

50

Learning God's Yes

When I was growing up, I believed in God without questioning what I really meant by this. God was God and that was that. At the age of three, my daughter reached about the same level of theological sophistication that I had achieved at a somewhat more advanced age. You'd ask her where God lives. She'd point to the sky and go on with her business.

In my case, more important than the existence of God was that of the goblins and evil spirits that lurked under my bed at ·night. About them I knew at least this much. When my mother turned on the light, got on her hands and knees, raised the bedspread, and looked under the bed, they were gone. When she turned off the light and left the room, they returned in force to haunt me.

In my early years, God figured in precisely the opposite fashion. When things were going well, when I did not need God, God was there. I believed in God without worrying too much about why. Yet when darkness fell and I was troubled, when I experienced what in later years would recur periodically as a dark night of the soul, I could not sense God anywhere.

So it was that I decided that if God did exist, God was not important to me. Other things were infinitely more so. I believed in what I could see, what I could touch, what I could learn, what I could love. Compared to these, the wonders of a

159

distant God in heaven held no allure. I found myself believing in the rainbow but not in the pot of gold at the end of it. If it did exist, it was not important to me. Or, more precisely, I knew enough, or thought I did, not to search for it, for such a search would be in vain. By the time I closed in, the rainbow would be gone.

None of this has changed. I still believe in the vanishing rainbow as I do in the dark sky over the mountains. But I also believe in God, and I believe that God is important to me. The God I believe in now is different from the God I did not believe in then. Here are some of the differences.

The God I believe in now does not intercede, like a royal eagle swooping down from on high, to save the day for those who, outnumbered and outflanked, fight under God's banner. To scale this down to size, the God I believe in is neither opposed to the new religious right nor bothered in the least by the lack of prayer in the public schools. Pray for rain and the God I believe in will not answer, whatever the change in the weather. And it makes no difference who is doing the praying, for the God I believe in does not play favorites when it comes to faith or creed. The God I believe in is not male or female or any divine combination of the two. All this I know, or think I know. On the other hand, I do not know, and will never know, just what the God I believe in is. The God I believe in will remain a mystery to me. It is hard to put into words, but let me share with you my own experience of the mystery of God.

If my theology is grounded anywhere, it is upon the principles of humility and openness. As to the first of these—and it may be a truism—the more I know life and death and God, the greater my ignorance appears. Beyond every ridge lies another slope and beyond every promontory looms yet another vast and awesome range. However far we trek, while cursed (or blessed) with the knowledge of our own mortality, we shall never finally know the answer to the question *why*. This, by the way, is one of the reasons I cannot embrace a rigidly dogmatic faith. Even should the dogma be fashioned wholly according to my own liking, experience tells me that it would not stand the test—my own test—of growth, unfolding truth and time.

This, then, is the lesson of humility. Alone, it is insufficient, teaching us only what we cannot hope to know. On the other hand, openness (the possibility principle), invites us to probe life as deeply as we can, without regard to limits. So it is that, accepting my smallness while remaining open to explore as fully as possible the unresolvable mystery of my own and our shared being, I find myself growing in faith. The mystery of life becomes ever more deep and wondrous, the gift of life ever more precious and unaccountable. By remaining open to the unknown, one dares to enter further into it. One grows in knowledge, yes, and in ignorance, but one also grows in wonder and, finally, in trust.

My own forays are usually journeys taken in meditation or prayer, but they also may come about through the medium of music, or nature, or some magical moment of human interaction. Losing oneself one finds oneself, and one's whole perspective is changed. Here words begin to fail me. I can only describe the experience as one of mystical union in that which is greater than all of its parts and yet present in each, that which gives meaning to all, beyond explanation, beyond knowing or naming.

The power which I cannot explain or know or name I call God. God is not God's name. God is my name for the mystery that looms within and arches beyond the limits of my being. Life force, spirit of life, ground of being, these too are names for the unnameable which I am now content to call my God.

When I pray to God, God's answer comes to me from within, not beyond. God's answer is yes, not to the specifics of my prayer but in response to my hunger for meaning and peace. God's answer is not a what or a how or a when or a why but a yes. *Choose life and trust life. Grow in service and love. Take nothing for granted. Be thankful for the gift. Suffer well. Dare to risk much. Consecrate your world with laughter and with tears. And know not what I am or who I am or how I am, know only that I am with you.* This is God's answer to my prayer.

As I plunge deeper, in fits and starts, seeking to penetrate the mystery of God, the mystery grows. It grows in wonder and in power, in moment and in depth. There are times when God is not with me, so many times. Times of distraction, fragmentation, alienation, brokenness. But when I open myself to God, incrementally my wholeness is restored. Perhaps that which I call the mystery of God is no more than the mystery of life itself. I cannot know, nor do I care, for the power that emanates from deep within the heart of this mystery is redemptive. It is divine. By opening myself to it, without ever hoping or presuming to understand it, I find peace.

The mystery of God will remain a mystery. That, I suppose, is as it should be. Anything less would fail to do justice to the everyday miracles of consciousness, of love and pain, of life and death. Responding to these miracles, responding to God's yes, I can do no other than to answer yes in return.

"Yes, I place my trust in Thee. Yes, I offer up my heartfelt thanks."

About the Author

F. Forrester Church is Amy Furth Church's husband, and father to Twig, who is ten, and Nina, who is seven. He is also Minister of the All Souls Unitarian Church in New York City; recipient of a Ph.D. in Church History from Harvard University; author of several books, including *Father & Son, The Devil & Dr. Church, Entertaining Angels,* and *The Seven Deadly Virtues,* all published by Harper & Row; and columnist, whose stories from life, "Fundamentals," appear weekly in the *Chicago Tribune.*